# TIDBITS®
## the book

All The News You Never Knew
That You Never Needed To Know ®

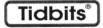

Published By
## Steele Media, Inc.
Billings, Montana

## Tidbits® The Book

is published by
Steele Media, Inc.
P.O. Box 1255
Billings, MT 59103
(406) 248-9000

The authors have gathered information in <u>Tidbits® The Book</u> from sources considered to be reliable; however, the accuracy of all information cannot be guaranteed.

You may obtain additional copies of this book from Steele Media, Inc., or directly from your local publisher of the Tidbits® paper.

Cover Design
Rob Johnson
Mission Graphics

Illustrators
D. Callahan
George Wenzel

Lithography
ABBAgraphics, Inc.

ISBN 0-966-3571-0-8
9 780966 357103

Printed in the United States of America

Dedicated to our Dads:

Lester Wilke, Sr.
July 11, 1910 — January 31, 1992

Rev. C.N. Steele
June 14, 1911 — May 5, 1985

They gave us life.
They gave us direction.
They gave us vision.

- David L. and Cecelia Steele

# ACKNOWLEDGMENTS

This book is possible because of the hard work and dedication of many key people who believe in Tidbits®. First of all we are grateful to Valmarie Darrington, Mona Lee McKown, Janice C. Walker and Kathy Wolfe who are free lance writers. We appreciate their hard work and dedication in finding obscure and interesting pieces of information. We want to thank our illustrators, D. Callahan and George Wenzel. To the employees at ABBAgraphics, Inc., Corky McKown, Patti Nixon, and Royce Ponessa, we thank you for the extra hours you put in to get this book printed. Thanks to Diane Gale of Diversified Management Assistance for proofreading. Many thanks to Jeanette White, our assistant at Steele Media, who keeps everything together for all of us. Last but not least we are grateful to publishers across the country of the Tidbits® paper, and to all their advertisers and readers. These are the real Tidbits® heroes.

# INTRODUCTION

A tidbit is defined as, *"a morsal of food to be devoured before the meal."* That's what Tidbits® is ...food for thought. The Tidbits paper is a weekly entertainment newspaper, devoted to publishing things you didn't know and distributed almost exclusively in restaurants. The Tidbits® paper is published by over one hundred forty independent publishers across the country. Tidbits® The Book is a compilation of 26 Tidbits® issues that were previously published in the Tidbits® paper.

Bon Appetit!

# Contents

# FABULOUS FIFTIES
by Kathy Wolfe

## Vital Statistics

- 1950: Newscaster Jane Pauley and singer Stevie Wonder were born. Edgar Rice Burroughs, author of 26 Tarzan of the Apes novels, died.
- 1951: Jane Seymour, star of Dr. Quinn, Medicine Woman, and TV's John Boy Walton star Richard Thomas were born. Publisher William Randolph Hearst died.
- 1952: Actors Christopher Reeve and Robin Williams were born. This was the year Eva "Evita" Peron, wife of Argentina President Juan Peron, died.
- 1953: In the year that model Christie Brinkley was born, Soviet dictator Joseph Stalin died.
- 1954: Talk show hosts Oprah Winfrey and Kathie Lee Gifford were born the year that actor Lionel Barrymore died.
- 1955: Russian gymnast Olga Korbut was born. Scientist Albert Einstein, famous for his theory of relativity, and Carmen Miranda, famous for her fruit-basket headdresses, died in 1955.
- 1956: Forrest Gump star Tom Hanks and actor/director Kevin Costner were born, along with basketball star Larry Bird. William Boeing, founder of Pacific Aero Products Company, now the Boeing Company, died.
- 1957: This was the year Princess Caroline of Monaco was born; and the year that Senator Joseph McCarthy died of cirrhosis of the liver, brought on by alcoholism.

- 1958: Singer Michael Jackson was born the same year that Pope Pius XII died.
- 1959: Tennis star John McEnroe was born, and Lou Costello, of comedy's Abbott & Costello team, died.

## They Tied The Knot

- Frank Sinatra and Ava Gardner wed in 1951, but divorced in 1957.
- In 1952, film actor Ronald Reagan married Nancy Davis.
- John F. Kennedy and Jacqueline Bouvier married in 1953.
- Baseball great Joe DiMaggio and actress Marilyn Monroe were married and divorced in 1954, after only nine months of marriage. Marilyn later married playwright Arthur Miller in 1956.
- Debbie Reynolds married Eddie Fisher in 1955. This union produced Carrie Fisher, who become famous as Princess Leia of Star Wars.
- Elizabeth Taylor divorced hotel magnate Conrad Hilton in 1951. She married Michael Wilding in 1952 and divorced him in 1957. Her next husband, Michael Todd, whom she married in 1957, was killed in an accident in 1958. She married Eddie Fisher in 1959.

## Around The World

- The population of the United States increased by about 28 million during the 1950's. 2,515,000 immigrants entered the U.S. Lifestyles changed during post-World War II prosperity, and the move to the suburbs began. Modern conveniences were in most American homes – televisions, washers, dryers, and dishwashers.
- In June of 1950, communist North Korean troops attacked South Korea, marking the beginning of the Korean War. Although 41 countries sent military equipment and supplies, it was the U.S. that provided over 90% of the troops and supplies. Approximately 2,180,000 were killed or wounded in the Korean War. General Douglas MacArthur led troops that were responsible for turning the war to the Allies' favor,

but President Truman removed him from command in April, 1951. This was because of MacArthur's continuing argument with government defense leaders over how the war should be won. MacArthur was in favor of "all-out victory," which included the bombing of China. Truman feared this would start World War III. The Korean War was the first war to have battles between jet aircraft. The U.S. lost more than 2,000 planes during the war. The truce ending the war was signed in July, 1953.

- The first color television became available in 1950.
- The minimum hourly wage rate in 1950 was 75¢ per hour.
- Charles Schulz began writing his "Peanuts" comic strip in 1950.
- In 1952, Princess Elizabeth of Great Britain became Queen Elizabeth II.
- In 1953, American citizens Julius and Ethel Rosenberg died in the electric chair, executed for spying for the Soviet Union during World War II. They were found guilty of passing atomic bomb secrets to the Soviet Union, and became the first Americans executed for wartime spying. Ethel's brother had previously worked at Los Alamos, New Mexico, the United States' atomic bomb production site. The Rosenbergs maintained their innocence to the bitter end.
- Former New Zealand book-keeper Edmund Hillary and Nepalese tribesman Tenzing Norgay became the first men to conquer the top of Mt. Everest, in 1953.

- 1954 marked the first year Veterans Day, November 11, was celebrated.
- In 1954, the U. S. Supreme Court outlawed segregation in U.S. schools.

- Disneyland theme park opened in Anaheim, CA, in 1955 at a cost of $17 million. The Disney animated feature films made in the 1950's were Cinderella ('50), Alice in Wonderland ('51), Peter Pan ('53), Lady and the Tramp ('55), and Sleeping Beauty ('59).
- Senator Joseph McCarthy of Wisconsin charged that Communists had secretly infiltrated the U.S. government, claiming a list of "57 card-carrying members of the Communist Party" in the State Department. He began investigations of several officials, which resulted in 36 days of televised hearings in 1954. Having no success in identifying any Communists' he was totally discredited.
- The first successful organ transplant, a kidney transplant, occurred in 1954.
- The first polio vaccine was declared safe and effective and made available for use in 1955. It was developed by Dr. Jonas Salk, the son of a New York City garment worker.
- In 1955, Rosa Parks refused to relinquish her bus seat to a white passenger in Montgomery, Alabama, an action which resulted in her arrest and spurred on the civil rights movement in the U.S. The law stated that whites and blacks were to sit in separate rows on the bus, and required that blacks relinquish seats in middle rows if all front seats were taken and whites wanted the middle seats. Dr. Martin Luther King, Jr. led a year-long boycott of the Montgomery bus system.
- Lego building blocks were introduced in 1955.
- The last trolleys in New York City ran in 1957.
- On October 4, 1957, the Soviet Union launched the first artificial satellite, Sputnik I, into orbit. The Russian meaning for Sputnik is "fellow traveler." Its flight ended three months later. The U.S. Army followed suit with Explorer I on January 31, 1958.
- The Vietnam War began in 1957, although most of the fighting done by the U.S. was not until 1965. The U.S. entered the war based on a policy established by President Harry Truman

that declared that the U.S. must provide aid to any nation threatened by Communists.

- A 1958 Gallup Poll declared Eleanor Roosevelt as the most admired woman in America.
- The Ford Motor Company produced Edsels from 1957 to 1959. The Edsel was named after Henry Ford's son.
- Two Presidents were in office during the 1950's – Harry Truman, who had been inaugurated in 1945 and served through 1952, and Dwight D. Eisenhower, who became President in 1953. Ike had been a World War II hero and president of Columbia University prior to his election. Truman had been a businessman, county judge, and U.S. Senator.
- Alaska became the 49th state in January, 1959, with Hawaii following as the 50th in August of that year.
- The Lincoln Memorial first appeared on the back of the penny in 1959. Prior to that, the words ONE CENT occupied this spot.

## Sports News

- Some of the baseball greats drafted into the Korean War were Whitey Ford, Ted Williams, and Willie Mays. It was Williams' second stint in wartime, having served three years as a Marine fighter pilot in World War II. Ted Williams returned to baseball in 1953, following 39 combat missions in Korea. He played the 37 games remaining in the season, and finished with a .407 batting average.
- 1951 was Joltin' Joe DiMaggio's final season in professional baseball, retiring from the New York Yankees. This year marked Mickey Mantle's first season with the team.
- 1951 marked the beginning of Hall of Famer Willie Mays' 22-year career. The 20-year-old was named the 1951 Rookie of the Year.
- At the 1952 Winter Olympics in Oslo, Norway, figure skater Dick Button won his second gold medal. He was the first to perform a triple-spin jump. Skier Andrea Mead Lawrence took two golds.
- Hank Aaron's 23-year baseball career began in 1954 with

the Milwaukee Braves.

- Yogi Berra was the league's Most Valuable Player for 1951, 1954, and 1955.
- Johnny Unitas signed on with the Baltimore Colts in 1956.
- Rocky Marciano was the world heavyweight boxing champion from 1952-1956. It was Floyd Patterson from 1956-1959.
- Roger Maris began his baseball career in 1957, with the Cleveland Indians. Two years prior to that, this Fargo, ND, native had changed his last name from Maras.
- Jackie Robinson, the first black in organized baseball, retired in 1957, with a lifetime batting average of .311.
- The 1958 baseball season marked the beginning of the migration of teams to the West Coast. The New York Giants moved to San Francisco, and the Brooklyn Dodgers headed for Los Angeles.
- Ed Lubanski bowled two 300 games in a row in June of 1959 at the Miami Bowling Palace.

## Books, Movies, And Television

- Some of the more notable films of the 1950's included *From Here to Eternity, Ben Hur, The Bridge Over the River Kwai, Gigi,* and *A Streetcar Named Desire.*
- Humphrey Bogart won the Best Actor Academy Award in 1951 for his role in *The African Queen.*
- Grace Kelly won Best Actress for *The Country Girl* in 1954.
- Marilyn Monroe burst on the Hollywood scene in the 1950's, with some of her more memorable roles in *Gentlemen Prefer Blondes, Seven-Year Itch,* and *Some Like It Hot.*
- Joanne Woodward's role in *The Three Faces of Eve,* about a young woman with multiple personalities, earned her the Oscar for Best Actress of 1957.
- Michael Orowitz appeared in the title role of *I Was A Teenage Werewolf* in 1957. Of course, he is better known as Michael Landon.
- James Dean became famous for his roles as a rebel, most

notably in *Rebel Without A Cause* ('55). His career was cut short when he was killed in a car accident in 1955 at age 24, after only three films.

- Eight *Ma & Pa Kettle* movies were produced during the 1950s.
- Some of the long-running television series that made their debut in the 1950's were *The Today Show* ('52), *The Tonight Show* ('54), *Captain Kangaroo* ('55), *Gunsmoke* ('55), *American Bandstand* ('57), *Lassie* ('54), and *The Lawrence Welk Show* ('55).
- The most popular TV series in 1954 was *I Love Lucy*. *Father Knows Best* first aired in 1954.
- Some of the other favorite series in the '50's included *Red Skelton, Art Linkletter, Leave It To Beaver, What's My Line?, The Ed Sullivan Show, Perry Mason, The $64,000 Question, Maverick*, and *Ozzie & Harriet*.
- Soap Operas that are still in production today that premiered in the 1950's are *The Guiding Light* ('52) and *As The World Turns* ('56).
- The Lennon Sisters made their television debut on *The Lawrence Welk Show* at Christmas of 1955.
- *The Guinness Book of Records* was published for the first time in 1955.
- *Charlotte's Web* came out in 1952, and Dr. Seuss' *Cat in the Hat* was published in 1957.
- Eight out of the 14 *James Bond* novels written by Ian Fleming were issued in the '50's.
- Other books we were reading in the '50's included *Exodus* ('59), *Peyton Place* ('56), *Dr. Zhivago* ('57), – which was banned in the Soviet Union, – and JFK's *Profiles in Courage* ('57).

## The Music Scene

- Patti Page had the top single hit for 1951 with "Tennessee Waltz".
- Elvis Presley made his television debut in 1956 on *Stage Show*, which starred the Dorsey Brothers. His first chart-

topping hit was "Heartbreak Hotel," in 1956. "Don't Be Cruel," "Hound Dog", and "Love Me Tender" came close behind that same year. His first starring role in a motion picture was *Love Me Tender* in 1956, which led to 32 other movies.

- Richard Penniman, also known as Little Richard, dazzled audiences with his wild and unusual performances, which influenced many performers that followed. His first hit was in 1955, "Tutti Frutti." He later retired from the music industry to pursue studies in the ministry.
- The first famous rock band was Bill Haley & The Comets, whose hit "Rock Around The Clock" was the theme song for a 1955 movie about juvenile delinquents. This didn't help the growing reputation of rock music as the music of rebellion.
- Buddy Holly and his band The Crickets hit the charts in 1957 with their first hit "That'll Be The Day." He soon followed solo with "Peggy Sue." He met an untimely death at age 22 in 1959 when he was killed in a plane crash, along with fellow stars Ritchie Valens and "The Big Bopper," J.P. Richardson.
- "Great Balls of Fire" pianist Jerry Lee Lewis scandalized the music industry in 1958 by marrying his 13-year-old cousin.
- "The Purple People Eater" was recorded in 1958 by Sheb Wooley, who later had a role in TV's "Rawhide."
- The Kingston Trio was established in 1958.
- Those folks who liked the mellower side of music preferred crooners Frankie Avalon, Pat Boone, and Bobby Darin, who had the top hit of 1959 , "Mack the Knife."

# 2

# WEATHER

by J. C. Walker

## Twister And Shout

- In spite of what you might think after seeing the spectacular special effects of recent disaster movies, a tornado draws air and debris INTO the funnel. Pitiful cows, trucks, farm equipment and bad guys would be pulled in rather than flung far and wide across the countryside. Winds blow toward the storm rather than away from it.

- A tornado happens when cold, dry air collides with warm, moist air and a rotating windstorm grows out of a thundercloud. Meteorologists estimate there are roughly 900 tornados a year in the U.S., with most occuring in "Tornado Alley" – Kansas, Oklahoma, Texas and South Dakota.

- Storm chasers beware: In spite of the glamour of following tornados as a hobby, in the U.S. tornados killed 29 people in 1995.

- Like everything else in California, tornados there are more laid back. The five to ten that occur annually rarely reach winds of 100 MPH, while those in Tornado Alley usually range between 200 and 300 MPH.

- One of the country's most spectacular tornados happened in St. Louis in 1896. The storm – or family of storms – tore a mile-long path across the city and Mississippi River docks. Fronted by a green cloud wall, the tornado then developed a horizontal funnel cloud that looked like a giant screw as it traveled over the city. Intense lightning flashed against a green, blue, purple, and yellow sky. Torrential rain started just after the funnel passed and continued for another day. St. Louis was demolished and at least 300 people died.

- Moviegoers at the opening of "Twister" in Circleville, Ohio, got more bang for their buck. Soaking rain penetrated the theater roof and caused the sudden collapse of the ceiling as the movie reached its disastrous crescendo. It was reported that customers received rain checks.

## Pictures At Eleven

- For many years people in England believed that the activity of bats could predict changes in the weather. Scientists there are now seriously studying the possibility. Since bats are totally blind and live in dark caves, it doesn't seem reasonable they would know about weather conditions, yet when weather is good and insects are flying, bats are out there dining and dashing. In lousy weather the bats stay home and hang out. Scientists believe there is a special membrane in the inner ear that signals changes in atmospheric pressure with resulting clear or stormy weather. The bat's metabolism changes in response to membrane changes, and depending on the message, they are either hungry and leave for dinner, or they are sleepy and stay home to catch a few bat Z's.
- Sunflowers also predict rain. They lift their flowers as air pressure drops and humidity increases in order to soak in more sun before rainclouds pass overhead.

## Wind Wizardry

- The power of the wind is especially evident in the Sahara Desert. Dunes formed by the wind there have been measured to heights of 1,400 feet, or as tall as the Empire State Building.

## Lightning Up

- The Earth is negatively charged; the atmosphere is positively charged. Lightning recharges the Earth's electrical field, which would fade away in about an hour otherwise.
- 2000 thunderstorms take place around the world at any given time. These result in roughly 30 to 100 cloud to

ground lightning strikes each second – about five million incidents of lightning a day worldwide.

- Lightning bolts are one to three inches wide.
- Lightning occurs in different ways. It can travel between points in a cloud, from a cloud to clear air, from a cloud to an adjacent cloud, and from a cloud to ground.
- Lightning can travel either up from earth to cloud or down from cloud to earth, often via an unlucky conductor. 200 people die every year as a result of lightning strikes.
- Lightning CAN strike the same place twice. Or three times. Or ...seven? Forest Ranger Roy C. Sullivan lost a toenail from the first strike and eyebrows in the second. The third time his hair caught on fire and in the fourth he sustained burns on his shoulder. The fifth – his hair was set on fire again and his legs were burned. The sixth he injured his ankle and the seventh time he went to the hospital with chest and stomach burns. Actually, the Guinness Book of World Records reports he is EX-Forest Ranger Roy C. Sullivan.

- Most lightning strikes have at least 3 or 4 secondary strikes, separated by 40 to 80 milliseconds.
- Lightning fertilizes the ground. Really! Since air is composed of four parts nitrogen to one part oxygen, when lightning strikes it deposits residual nitrogen in the soil.

## Shine On

- Special events are planned in Barrow, Alaska, early in May - that's when the sun comes up after 67 days without sunshine.

Summer lasts - without a sunset or darkness - until early in August. In 1996 the weather cooperated on the first day of summer with a record-tying high temperature of 36 degrees.

- Yuma, Arizona, has the most sunshine of any location in the United States. The sun shines there 91 per cent of daylight hours, or 4,055 hours a year.

## Foggy Bottom

- London's "pea soup" fog of the Sherlock Holmes' novels may have been loaded with ambiance, but it was also loaded with pollutants, too. It literally was "pea green" because of the green smoke emitted by the coal-burning factories. Londoners finally came to their senses in 1952 when an unbelievable 4,000 people died from toxic fumes in one incident and restrictions were issued on coal use.

## But It's A Dry Heat

- The highest shade temperature ever recorded is 136 degrees Farenheit at Al'Aziziyah, Libya, on September 13, 1922.

## Do Not Enter When Flooded

- Floods kill more people every year than hurricanes, tornados, wind, or lightning combined.

## For The Hail Of It

- The larger the hail stones, the greater the destruction. Seems reasonable, doesn't it? However, the reason a larger sized hail stone can wreak so much havoc is not only because of its size, but because it falls with greater force. Tiny pellets don't do much more than make noise, but golf-ball sized hail travels at 50 MPH when it hits the ground. Hail three inches in diameter is estimated to move at 60 MPH and grapefruit-sized lands at 100 MPH or more.

## Clouds In My Coffee

- Low, dense cloud formations reflect heat from the sun and usually mean cooler weather. High clouds let the sun's radiation through and trap infrared radiation from the Earth's surface. These clouds almost always signal a warming trend.

## Summertime Blues

- The explosion of volcanic island Krakatoa in Indonesia in 1883 not only spewed ash and pumice more than 4,000 miles, but changed major weather patterns of the world for years. At first, Europeans and Americans were treated to breathtaking red and gold sunsets in the months that followed, but they were in for an unpleasant surprise. Ash high in the atmosphere blocked the sun and triggered unusual amounts of rain and snow long after the island disappeared from the map, resulting in unseasonable blizzards. 1884 was known as "The Year Without a Summer."

## Mildew Not A Problem

- The Atacama Desert in northern Chile has received no rainfall in the history of weather recordkeeping. An occasional cloud burst will fall on a very limited area and the moisture evaporates as soon as it hits the ground.

## Get Out Those Board Games

- Mt. Wai-'ale-'ale on Kauai, Hawaii, has 350 rainy days a year.

## Me And My Shadow

- Punxsutawney Phil in Pennsylvania may have the American franchise on winter weather predictions, but we have a sneaking suspicion he may have borrowed the concept from an old English rhyme. By odd coincidence, February 2 was known as Candlemas Day, the day in which all sorts of predictions were made about the year to come. As for six more weeks of winter, the verse is:

  If Candlemas Day be fair and bright,
  Winter will have another flight;
  But if it be dark with clouds and rain,
  Winter is gone and will not come again.

## Hot Stuff

- In summer, 1990, a heat wave in Phoenix, Arizona, brought the city to a standstill. One TV station's thermometer recorded a high of 124 degrees Farenheit. Especially hard hit was the airport, where Boeing 737's were grounded because the charts used to calculate takeoff distance didn't go above 120. The runways were also melting.

## Snow Foolin'

- The snowiest season on record in the U.S. was at Paradise, Mt. Rainier, Washington. 1,224-1/2 inches of snow fell between February 19, 1971 and February 18, 1972.

## Hurricane Hits

- Hurricanes are also called typhoons and tropical cyclones.
- The practice of naming hurricanes began during World War II, when military meteorogists communicated over long distances and had to be sure they were talking about the same storms. They named the hurricanes after wives and sweethearts – men got equal time in 1978 when storms were alternately named with male and female tags. Every year storms are named in alphabetical order, with a predetermined list of English, Spanish, or Hawaiian names already chosen depending on the region.
- A really nasty hurricane can have its name retired like an athlete's jersey number. Names destined not to be used again are Agnes, Alicia, Allen, Andrew, Anita, Audrey, Betsy, Beulah, Bob, Camille, Carla, Carmen, Carol, Celia, Cleo, Connie, David, Diana, Diane, Donna, Dora, Edna, Elena, Eloise, Fifi, Flora, Frederic, Gilbert, Gloria, Gracie, Hattie, Hazel, Hilda, Hugo, Inez, Ione, Janet, Joan, and Klaus.
- In the northern hemisphere, hurricanes rotate from left to right – in the southern, from right to left.
- The most rainfall produced by a hurricane was 71.8 inches in 24 hours by Hurricane Denise in January, 1966, at Foc-Foc, La Reunion Island in the Indian Ocean.
- The biggest hurricane on record is Typhoon Tip in the Northwest Pacific in 1979. It was 1100 kilometers wide. The smallest hurricane on record is Tropical Cyclone Tracy, 50 kilometers wide, in Darwin, Australia, in 1974.
- The longest hurricane on the books is Hurricane John, which occurred during the summer in 1994. It ambled across the

Northeast and Northwest Pacific for 31 days. It was renamed Typhoon John and then Hurricane John again as it meandered back and forth across the International Date Line.

- Two hurricanes share the "honors" as the most destructive. The most damage was caused by Hurricane Andrew in the Bahamas, Florida, and Louisiana in 1992 – estimates are there may have been as much as 25 to 35 BILLION dollars in damages. The worst death toll was in the Bangladesh Cyclone of 1970 in which at least 300,000 people were lost.
- Hurricanes die out over land masses, not because of the "friction" but because there is no source of moisture to fuel them. Hurricane Andrew may have been so destructive because the storm's path was across swamps and inlets, fortifying the hurricane rather than weakening it.
- Hurricane Andrew not only devastated human life and property, but may have wiped out animal species too. Only 17 of the rare wild Shaus swallowtail butterfly remained on Elliot Key in southern Florida after Andrew struck. Fortunately, a scientist was studying the insect and had 100 eggs incubating in his kitchen at the time, and those eggs and the remaining critters were bred to bring back the species.
- On an average globally, hurricanes occur most frequently during September and least often during May.

# AUTOMOBILES
By Mona McKown

- Definition: usually a 4-wheel automotive vehicle designed for passenger transportation on streets and roadways and commonly propelled by an internal-combustion engine using a volatile fuel.
- No one person can be called the inventor of the automobile. It is the culmination of many ideas by many individuals. However, the first self-propelled land vehicle that had an engine was built by Nicholas Cugot, a Frenchman, in 1769. It was a bulky three-wheeled cart powered by a huge steam engine. It could travel at a speed of three miles an hour and had to be refueled every 15 miles.
- In 1789, Oliver Evans received the first United States patent for a self-propelled carriage. It was a wagon with four wheels and a paddle wheel at the rear. The paddle wheel enabled the vehicle to operate on either land or in the water. This vehicle weighed a mere 21 tons!
- Karl Benz of Mannheim, Germany, at the age of 34, began work on a motorized tricycle. It was the first automobile powered by an internal combustion engine. The tricycle was water-cooled and its first demonstration was in 1885, through the streets of Mannheim. Benz sold his first car to Emile Roger of Paris, two years later. Roger then opened a Benz franchise in Paris. In 1893, he added a fourth wheel, for stability. By the end of the century, Benz autos were traveling up and down the steepest hills and going at speeds up to 14 miles per hour.

- On June 11, 1895, the first auto race for gasoline-powered cars was held in Paris . The course was a 732-mile round trip between Paris and Bordeaux. The fastest car was later disqualified because it was a two-seater Panhard-Levasson. The winner was then declared to be a Mr. Koechlin, who was driving a Peugeot.
- William C. Durant, who owned the Buick Motor Company, merged with Cadillac, Oldsmobile, Oakland (which was later called Pontiac), and Chevrolet plus some lesser auto firms to form General Motors, in 1908.
- In 1910, Barney Oldfield, an auto racer, set a new speed record at Daytona Beach, Florida. The new record was 131.724 miles per hour.

## Auto Firsts

- In 1887 the first gasoline-powered automobile was put on the road by a German named Gottlieb Daimler.
- The first successful American gasoline-powered automobile was built by the Duryea brothers, Frank and Charles. Their vehicle was called "a horseless buggy" and appeared on the scene in either 1892 or 1893.
- The first air-conditioned automobile was manufactured by Packard Motor Car Company in Detroit, Michigan, in 1939. The air was cooled to the temperature desired, dehumidified, filtered, and circulated. The refrigerating coils were behind the rear seat in an air duct. Heat was provided in the winter with heating coils in a different compartment but in the same air duct.
- The first automobile accident occurred between Henry Wells of Springfield, Massachusetts, in a Duryea Motor Wagon and Evylyn Thomas, who was riding a bicycle, on May 30, 1896, in New York City. Evylyn was taken to the hospital with a broken leg and Henry spent the night in jail, waiting to hear the extent of Evylyn's injuries.
- Henry H. Bliss, age 68, of New York City, was the first automobile fatality. On September 13, 1899, he was knocked

down and run over as he was getting off a streetcar at Central Park West. He was taken to the hospital where he died. The driver, Arthur Smith, was arrested and held with $1,000 bail.

- In 1901, New York State required the first automobile license plates. Under "an act to amend the highway law, in relation to the use of highways by automobiles or motor vehicles," owners were required to register their vehicles within 30 days. The owners had to give a description of their vehicles along with their name and address. The fee for registration was $1.00. In 1901, the fees received totaled $954 and increased to $1,082 in 1902. The license plates were required to be over 3 inches high and had the owner's initials on them.

- Jacob German, who was the operator of Cab No. 1,565 for the Electric Vehicle Company, was the first man arrested for speeding. On May 20, 1899, German was driving 12 mph on Lexington Avenue, New York City. He was booked and jailed.

- The first drive-in service station was opened by the Gulf Refining Company on December 1, 1913, in Pittsburgh, Pennsylvania. The station provided free crankcase service and remained open all night.

- The 1987 Lincoln Town Car was the first American car to offer a factory-installed CD player as an option.

## Quotes For Driving

- "Thanks to the interstate highway system, it is now possible to travel across the country from coast to coast without seeing anything." – Charles Kuralt, *On the Road* 1985

- "Americans are broad-minded people. They'll accept the fact that a person can be an alcoholic, a dope fiend, a wife beater, and even a newspaperman, but if a man doesn't drive, there is something wrong with him." – Art Buchwald, *How Much Is That Dollar Worth* 1961

## What's In A Name

- Three men, T. S. Fauntleroy, H. R. Averill, and E. H. Lowe, all of Chicago, formed an automotive firm in 1909. They could not settle on a name for their vehicle so when production began they called it "the Car Without a Name." This name stuck until 1910, when they changed it to F. A. L., using their initials. The production continued until 1914.

- Between the years of 1917 and 1918, L. L. Allen, of Willoughly, Ohio, produced about forty cars with the dramatic name of "Ben Hur."
- In 1915, the Madison Motor Company of Anderson, Indiana, named their first car "Dolly Madison" as a tribute to the late First Lady of the United States. However, they didn't do quite enough research, as President Madison's wife spelled her name "Dolley." Later the motor company changed the name to "Madison." They remained in production until 1919.
- The Orson, which was more popularly known as "the Millionaires's Car," was built in 1911, in Springfield, Massachusetts. The company was backed by 100 of the most prominent bankers in New York City. The 100 bankers were to take delivery of the first 100 vehicles. Financial mismanagement and expensive lawsuits caused the company to go under within two years.
- Fred Pickle built an unusual-looking car in 1906. It was built in Greenville, Michigan. It used ordinary bicycle wheels and a small three-and-a-half horsepower engine. Its name was "the Pickle" after its inventor.
- The "Tin Lizzie" was the name given to Henry Ford's Model T. This car was the first "people's car." Ford declared, "I'm going to democratize the automobile and when I'm through, everybody will be able to afford one and about everybody will have one." In 1908, when production first began, the price was $850. Thereafter, the price dropped each year until 1923, when it cost $290. Ford sold 15.8 million Model T's between 1908 and 1927. The Model T was built with the idea of not only being an inexpensive car but also a well-built car. It offered a four-cylinder, twenty-horsepower motor, a revolutionary planetary transmission and a high-riding vanadium steel body with four sturdy wheels.

• In April of 1933, Adolf Hitler wanted a car for every German – a "people's car." He met Ferdinand Porsche, a self-educated engineer. Ferdinand's idols were Thomas Edison and Henry Ford and, like them, he believed in spreading technology to both the rich and the poor. On January 17, 1934, Porsche sent a car design to Hitler. A few months later, he was called to a secret meeting with Hitler in Berlin. After the short meeting (about 15 minutes) Hitler decided to open the world's biggest automobile plant to produce his "people's car." Hitler directed Porsche to start work immediately and told him that the car must sell for 1,000 Reichsmarks (which was about $250), the current price of a medium-sized German motorcycle. Porsche was supposed to receive help from the Reich Motor Industries Organization, the RMIO.

However, RMIO - Mercedes-Benz, Opel and others – wanted their executives in charge, not Porsche. The RMIO

ordered Porsche to build three running prototypes in ten months, which they knew was impossible. Porsche, of course, missed the deadline. The RMIO then notified Hitler, expecting that Porsche would get into trouble because he had not met the deadline. Their plan backfired, however, and in 1935, the car makers sent out a memo stating: "that they had decided to build 'the people's car' as a common effort. Porsche soon had all the help he needed.

The price of 1,000-marks was still impossible. To help cut costs, Porsche designed a two-cylinder engine but it failed. He then assigned the task of creating a workable engine to Franz Reimspeiss, who was an employee. In forty-eight hours, Reimspeiss drew up a four-cylinder, horizontally opposed engine. The four-cylinder proved to be cheaper to mass-produce than the two-cylinder. On May 26, 1938, Hitler laid the cornerstone for the world's largest auto assembly plant under one roof. The car was named "the Strength-Through-Joy Motor Car" or *Kraft-durch-Freude* in German. This was later shorten to the KdF car.

Every German could own a KdF car, through a government saving-plan. The plan enabled the workers to have 5 marks per week deducted from their pay and deposited in a special KdF-car bank account. This scheme collected more than $68 million, which later disappeared.

In 1935, when Germany surrendered during World War II, Porsche was briefly arrested as a war criminal. After his release, he pursued another dream – a two-seated, rear-engine sports car.

Porsche lived long enough to see more than 50,000 of his "people's cars" produced. He died on New Year's Day, 1951, at the age of seventy-five. The production of his car continued in different plants around the world. In 1994 the total production of these cars was more than 21 million. The "people's car" of Porsche's design is known today as the Bug, Beetle, or Volkswagen.

• Identical twin brothers, Francis and Freelan Stanley, from New England, were the creators of the Stanley Steamer. They ran a successful manufacturing business for dry photographic plates. They decided they would like to produce a well-made car after they saw a poorly-made one at a fair. The Stanley brothers chose steam for a source of power as there were already a growing number of automobiles powered in this way. The internal combustion engine was very complicated; it had to be hand cranked to start and was very smelly. Electric cars needed to be recharged so often that they were very inconvenient. The Stanley vehicles were very simple, with only 15 moving parts in the engines, and required no transmission, clutch, spark plugs or gear shift. Under a full head of steam the automobile could travel up to 150 mph, quietly and with very little pollution.

The problem with the Stanley Steamer was not with the car itself, but with the inventors of it. The Stanley brothers were not overly business-oriented. Therefore, the small factory produced only 1,000 cars annually. They spent hardly anything on advertising and they resisted style changes, written guarantees, and down payments. The brothers were also very choosy about to whom they sold a Stanley Steamer.

They were, however, setting speed records in many trial races. In 1906, a Stanley reached the incredible speed of 127.66 mph, which for that time was most amazing.

Francis and Freelan were quite content with the way things were going but the competitors were not. The competition began supplying fresh objections to the public as to the safety of the Stanley Steamer, and the new developments to the internal-combustion engine were making use of the steam engine expensive and old-fashioned. The Stanley Steamer was produced from 1897-1925.

## The Last Look

- In 1994 there were 175,128,000 licensed drivers of motor vehicles in the United States. Of those drivers, 51% were males and 49% were females.
- In 1994 male drivers were involved in more fatal accidents than female drivers. There were about 38,200 men and 14,600 women involved in those fatal accidents.
- The most popular colors for vehicles in 1994 included white for small trucks and vans, white for sports cars, green for full-size cars, and green for luxury cars.
- The 6 most popular kinds of cars for 1994, in order of popularity, were Ford Taurus, Honda Accord, Ford Escort, Toyota Camry, Saturn, and Honda Civic.

# ODD THINGS

By V.B. Darrington

## Animal Oddities

- Talk about lazy! The cowbird won't even raise its own kids! It leaves its egg in another bird's nest. When the egg hatches, the young cowbird promptly pushes any other eggs or hatchlings out of the nest. The impostor then takes advantage of his unwitting foster parents, who supply him with all the food he needs. As the young cowbird freeloads, he often grows much larger than his adoptive parents.
- According to the British press, one thousand pigs on a farm in Wiltshire, England, went on a rampage. The raging horde broke from their pens and ate 1,120 pounds of cattle food, electric wires, wooden gates, 2-1/2 tons of hay, 30 asbestos sheets, three acres of pasture, and parts of a light airplane!
- In a single leap, a flea can propel itself 150 times its length and 80 times its height. If an adult human could accomplish this same feat, he would be able to jump more than 400 feet in the air and cover over 300 yards before touching the ground (he could also negotiate a very lucrative NBA contract)!
- Inhabitants of the African Congo basin use "Driver" ants as living sutures. When a native suffers a cut, he holds one of the large ants to the wound and coaxes the creature to bite. The ant's jaws clamp the edges of the wound together, and the body of the ant is then pinched off. The head and jaws are left in place while the wound heals together.
- Turkeys are too stupid to come in out of the rain. Domestic

turkeys are so easily confused that they will often panic in a rainstorm. Turkeys have been known to look up at the storm until their sinuses fill with rain. The poor animals then catch pneumonia – or even drown on dry land. But rain isn't the only problem. Turkeys have on occasion become so frightened by airplanes, barking dogs, or back-firing cars that they have scrambled into the corner of their pen and smothered each other in the swarm.

- The Cal Ripken of horses: An American dray horse never took a vacation in 8,545 days. The horse pulled a dairy wagon every morning – covering a total of 102,540 miles.
- The California sea otter feeds while floating on its back. The otter collects crabs and sea-urchins from the ocean floor and then brings them to the surface. The otter places a rock on his stomach, and then backfloats casually, cracking the shellfish on the rock – using its stomach for a picnic table.
- Scientists, studying the eating habits of elephants, baked bits of automobile tires into loaves of bread to see what the elephants would do. They didn't notice.
- Ten days after her eggs hatch, a mother octopus dies of starvation.
- Angler fish are able to stretch their stomachs to swallow other fish twice their own size. Imagine eating a twelve-foot submarine sandwich.
- Americans spend over $3 billion each year on dog and cat food.
- *The Providence Journal Bulletin* reported the odd attack of a ferocious squirrel. At a real estate office in Kirkland, Washington, a squirrel somehow entered the building and held more than 50 employees hostage. Whenever any of them attempted to leave, the squirrel would rush forward and attack them. So, the employees stood cowering against the wall holding their jackets and empty boxes between them and the squirrel. Finally, someone called 911. Officer Steve Oskierko arrived on the scene. He promptly had to call in backup when he split his pants while trying to corner the crazed animal. Eventually replacements arrived with new pants for Officer

Oskierko. He captured the squirrel and took it to a veterinarian to test it for rabies. But the squirrel was not so easily defeated. He gnawed through his cage, attacked the vet and his office staff, and escaped into the woods. The squirrel is still at-large.

- The fishermen of Normandy have a time-honored custom to ensure the bounty of the fishing harvest. When they catch the first fish of the season, they don't keep it – they get it drunk! They pour half a bottle of wine down its throat and throw it back. They believe the other fish will crowd around the returning fish, smell the wine, and then spend the rest of the season trying to get caught!

## Take This Job And...

- In the course of a normal day's work, a typist's fingers might cover as much as 12 miles.
- The newspaper ad for prospective Pony Express riders read as follows: "Wanted: Young, skinny fellows, not over 18. Must be expert riders willing to risk death daily. Orphans preferred. Wages $25 per week. Apply Central Overland Express."
- British hospital attendants are sometimes on duty 133 hours or more per week.
- There are over 40,000 members of the actor's union, the Screen Actors Guild, in the United States but only about 14% make over $3,000 a year.
- The newsboys had to be musclemen when they delivered the Sunday New York Times on October 17, 1965. It was almost a thousand pages long and weighed seven-and-a-half pounds a copy!

## Sports

- A junior high school basketball player was the high scorer for both sides. Ted Kern, of Terre Haute, Indiana, led his team to a 13-2 victory, and he scored the only basket for the opposing team.
- Daniel O'Leary got so excited when he hit his first home run that he actually ran the bases backwards. The score was tied at the time and hapless Dan was called out.

- The Sugarloaf Mountain Ski Resort in Maine held a Heavyweight Ski Contest. The minimum weight of entrants was 250 pounds, and there was a special category for anyone weighing in at over 400 pounds.
- All-state football running back, William "Butch" Lindsay, was the winner of his West Virginia high school's "1977 Homemaker of the Year Award." He was the highest scorer on the written test.
- The college athletic scouts went crazy when a printing error listed Bobby Kilgore of Central High School in Omaha, Nebraska, as 6 feet 11 inches. That made him the fourth tallest senior in the country. The recruiting invitations poured in from colleges all over the country. But Bobby turned them all down. The program listing was a typo–Bobby was unfortunately just 6 feet tall.
- When Hank Aaron broke Babe Ruth's home-run record, he received more than 900,000 fan letters – not one of them was from his mailman!

## It's My Body And I'll Cry If I Want To

- In 1960, North Americans were eating diets that were forty per cent fat. In recent years, that number has fallen to thirty-four per cent – and cholesterol levels have fallen along with fat intake. Surprisingly, the weight of an average young American (between the ages of 25 and 30) has risen ten pounds since1986.
- If you hold back a sneeze you could tear a muscle in your face or cause a nosebleed or a stroke.
- Your chances of having a bad dream increase in direct proportion to the decrease of your bedroom temperature.
- A 17-year-old Florida girl sneezed for 155 days. Doctors finally resorted to shock treatments to stop the sneezing.
- In 1797, Claude Ambroise Seurat was born looking normal and healthy. By the time he was an adult, Claude's back-to-chest thickness was only three inches, one inch less that the measurement of his puny biceps. He went on to live a normal

life and became rich exhibiting himself around Europe.

- Almost 20 million Americans don't have a single tooth in their mouth.
- A young wife in York, England, is allergic to her husband. When he kisses her, the area around her lips gets red and itchy.
- It was believed that the heart, not the brain, was the center of learning. That's where we get the saying, "To learn by heart."

## Biggest Of The Big

- With the invention of the electric elevator in 1887, the title of "World's Tallest Building" passed quickly to taller and taller buildings. The 612-foot Singer Building in New York was the tallest for only a few months until the 700-foot Metropolitan Life Building was completed. The Woolworth Building became the tallest in 1913 at 792 feet. Then in 1931, the first building with over 100 stories was built. It was the Empire State Building in New York City. It had 102 stories and was 1,250 feet tall. In the early seventies, two twin towers of the World Trade Center surpassed that record with 110 stories and 1,350 feet. The title of world's tallest building is now held by Chicago's Sears tower which stands 1,450 feet tall.
- The tallest living things on our planet are the Redwoods, which can achieve a height of 340-feet, as high as a 30-story building, with a girth of 25 feet. It is believed that some of these trees are over 4,000 years old. The bark of these trees is largely resistant to fire, fungus, decay, and insect infestation. No wonder they stay around so long!
- The Earth gains weight everyday. Each day as much as 10 tons of cosmic debris seep through our atmosphere and settle to earth.
- The entire current population of the Earth could fit into a box measuring one mile square. However, if the population of

the Earth continues to double every 37 years, in 900 years there will be 30 million billion people! Each square yard of the Earth's surface will have to accommodate 100 people.

## There Hadn't Ought To Be A Law

- An old law in Colorado Springs, Colorado, gives a dog the right to one bite.
- In Minnesota, men's and women's undergarments are not allowed to hang on the same clothesline.
- Even if you want to, you can't wear roller skates in a public lavatory in Portland, Oregon.
- Carriage horses in New Orleans must wear diapers.

- You'll be arrested if you tie your crocodile to a fire hydrant in Michigan.

## Lost In Space

- Where does all the lost airline luggage go? To the unclaimed baggage center in Scottsboro, Alabama. The missing luggage is then periodically auctioned. Some lucky people have been able to find their own missing items and buy them back.
- The obvious reason that no one has seen Santa Claus is because he is so darn fast! Two students at the University of Chicago computed the math on Santa's Christmas Eve visits to children of the world. Since there are more than 2 billion

homes on his delivery route, Santa and his reindeer need to cover about 100 million miles. So, if Santa follows the rotation of the Earth, and thereby allows himself 24 hours of night, he still has time to spend only 1/20,000 of a second in each home, with only 1/2 hour left for travel time.

- The Voyager spacecrafts launched by NASA carry small gold placards depicting an image of a man and a woman, a map to planet Earth, and a variety of other information about man and our planet. It is predicted that in 100,000 years, the first Voyager craft will arrive at the nearest star. In the event that the craft is intercepted by aliens, they will be treated to a depiction of mankind in the 20th century, in a time as far distant from us as we are now from Neanderthal man.

## Overstated

- Editor of the <u>London Times</u> "Crossword," Edward Akenhead included the word, <u>honorificabilitudinitatibus</u> in a puzzle.
- Marva Drew of Iowa spent 6 years typing the numbers 1 to 1,000,000 on a standard typewriter, filling close to 2,500 pages.
- If you wanted to write the longest word in the English language, you would write the chemical term describing Bovine NADP – specific glutamate dehydrogenase. You would need 3,600 letters. Do you still want to?
- The name of a hill in the North Island district of New Zealand is Taumatawhakatangihangakoauaoutamateaturipukakap-ikmungahoronukupokaiwhenuakitanatahu. This means "the Place where Tamatea, the man with the big knee who slid, climbed, and swallowed mountains, known as Land-eater, played on his flute to his loved one."
- The English instructions found in a rental car in Japan stated, "When a passenger of foot heave in sight, tootle the horn. Trumpet at him melodiously first, but if he still obstacles your passage, then tootle him with vigor."

# OCEANS AND BEACHES
by J.C. Walker

- Because they exist entirely under water many of the world's geographical superlatives have never been viewed by human beings. The world's longest mountain range is 46,000 miles long, four times as long as the Andes, Rockies, and Himalayans put together. The Mid-Ocean Ridge rings the world's oceans like a giant seam.
- The tallest mountain in the United States lies off the coast of Hawaii. Mauna Kea, measured from the ocean floor, is 33,465 feet high.
- The world's longest waterfall is located under the Denmark Strait between Iceland and Greenland. While the idea of an underwater waterfall sounds a little odd, what happens is that a slow current of much colder water travels down a cliff face into the depths of the ocean. This current travels over 2.2 miles, more than three times farther than the tallest "dry" waterfall in Venezuela, Angel Falls.

## Smokin'!

- If there were competition for Weirdest Creature on Earth, a strong candidate would undoubtably be an underwater contender called the Vent Worm. Discovered by scientists in 1977, when deep sea volcanic eruptions were being studied for the first time, Vent Worms are more than just underwater pretty faces. The large ones grow to lengths of four to eight feet, attach their wormy "feet" to the deep ocean bottom and sprout feathery red plumes from their tops, which sway in ocean currents like trees. While these creatures are considered rare, whole colonies can surround a new magma vent within a year or two of its eruption. The fact that they can grow as much as 33 inches a year is remarkable. Even more fascinating to scientists was that the pitch-black vent world has a whole new way of earning an underwater living. They discovered that specially evolved bacteria thrive on the sulphur-laden hot water emitted from the vents, and that they had adapted to using sulphur, not sunlight, to produce their own food. The giant Vent Worms have no digestive system to absorb these bacteria – their internal tissues simply provide a place for the bacteria to live and produce food on which the worms live.

## Whale Of A Tale

- Peruvian scientists discovered a previously unknown type of whale in 1991. The critters had been caught by fisherman for many years, but the 12-foot Beaked Whale has never been seen alive. It dives deep, lives well out to sea, and stays submerged up to an hour at a time.

## The Pressure's On

- Never let it be said that those deep-sea divers don't have a sense of humor. They decorate styrofoam cups and attach them to the outside of deep-water research submarines. At 3,000 to 9,000 pounds per-square-inch, the water pressure squeezes every bit of air out of the cups and turns them into teeny-weeny dive souvenirs.

## All Tide Up

- The greatest tidal changes occur in the Bay of Fundy in Nova Scotia, Canada. In spring, tides may range as much as 47 feet in depth. Tahiti has almost no tidal changes at all.

## Deep Thoughts

- The lowest point on earth is the Mariana Trench, off the coast of Guam, which plunges to 35,802 feet below sea level.
- Almost all the deep oceans maintain average temperatures only several degrees above freezing.
- Sunlight dims by one-tenth for every 250 feet of water depth.

At 1600 feet, human beings have just barely enough light to see, since the light has about one-millionth the intensity of that on the water's surface.

## Current Events

- While we may think that the sea carries away all our pollution and other unpleasantness, ocean currents really do circulate around the world. When deep water forms in the the North Atlantic Ocean, it sinks, travels south and circulates around Antarctica, then travels upward to the Indian and Pacific Oceans and back to the Atlantic basin. Scientists estimate it may take a thousand years for water to journey from the North Atlantic to the North Pacific.

- Surface currents move in large, slow circles called gyres. Gyres were hot news when a variety of ocean-going articles were washed overboard in heavy seas.

- In 1990, 60,000 pairs of Nike shoes were dumped in the northeastern Pacific. Six months later, shoes washed up on the shores of British Columbia, Washington, and Oregon. Shoe scavengers held swap meets to reunite mated pairs. Three years after the disaster, shoes began bobbling onto beaches in Hawaii. Scientists estimate their next stop will be in Japan and the Phillipines, and by 1997 the last remaining Nike voyagers may turn up again on North American shorelines.

- Then in 1992, 29,000 plastic tub toys also decided to "just do it." Also lost at sea in the Pacific, duckies, turtles, beavers, and froggies began to appear ten months later on the beach in Sitka, Alaska. Scientists expect to find them eventually around the Arctic, North Pacific and, someday, the northern North Atlantic.

## Club Meddies

- Fast-moving whirlpools are underwater versions of hurricanes. Called "meddies," most develop thousands of feet down in the Mediterrean Sea before moving into the Atlantic Ocean. Some may be as much as 100 kilometers wide and 800 meters deep. Temperatures within the "eye" are 4C warmer and at the core the water is significantly saltier than outside. Meddies have been tracked all over the world – scientists followed one for 2000 kilometers over a two-year period.

## Hot Stuff

- The world's largest volcano field was discovered by satellite in 1993. Over 1100 volcanoes in an area the size of upstate New York were revealed at the bottom of the mid-eastern Pacific Ocean.

## Slug Fest

- One of the best-keep secrets of oceanographers is the devoted following of the unusual sea creatures called nudibranchs. Otherwise known as sea slugs, nudibranchs come in a dazzling array of colors, sizes, and adaptations. While these beasts may seem to swim about at the mercy of their more fercious oceanic counterparts, in truth, a mouthfull of nudibranch carries such a wallop that most carnivores avoid them. Scientists think the slugs eat the venomous parts of similarly nasty coral polyps, anemones, and sponges, incorporating the sting into their own systems. Some even emit sulfuric acids. Underwater photographers love finding nudibranches during dives, but these guys don't make it easy – several types look exactly like the kelp in which they live. The Clown Nudibranch is white and covered with red and yellow polka dots.

## Kids, Don't Try This At Home

- The world's record for longest underwater breath-holding goes to Francisco "Pepin" Ferreras off the Grand Bahama Islands on November 14, 1993. He held his breath for 2 minutes, 9 seconds.

## A Soggy Hubbell

- A decommissioned Navy suveillance post is being used as an underwater telescope of sorts. The Point Sur Naval Facility closed its acoustical tracking program in 1986, but scientists are using the "hydrophone array" like astronomers use telescopes. While images are visible for only scores of feet even at the surface, in the ocean sound travels literally thousands of miles. Scientists are listening for evidence of nuclear testing, marine mammal migrations, and earthquakes all over the earth's underwater surface.

## Where No One Has Gone Before

- There are reports of oceanographers developing plans for underwater space stations on continental shelves near Long Island Sound and the Molokai Channel in Hawaii. Funded by independent financiers rather than the government, the ocean bases will provide facilities with which to study and experiment within the ocean ecosystems. Teams of as many as 30 persons will live in the stations at a time, and visitors will be invited to tour underwater.

## And After This, Mind Probes

- Scientists are actually working on force-field technology to repel sharks from human-occupied areas. They've tried odors, tapes of killer whales, and dyes, all with unremarkable success. What seem to work, however, are electrical impulses that offend shark sensibilities and convince them that the bearer is not a tasty seal or fish morsel. The electrical impulse gizmo is called a "Protective Ocean Device" or POD. Scientists predict that, when perfected, the instrument can be installed in life jackets and surfboards, and on cables which will replace the nets now killing thousands of marine animals at beaches and harbors.

## No Jelly Baby

- The largest jellyfish ever discovered was in Massachusetts Bay. The "bell" of the critter was 7-feet wide and the longest tentacle measured 120 feet.

## Worst Idea Of The Month Award

- The North Carolina Museum of Natural Sciences recently unveiled its latest acquisition: the teeth of a prehistoric shark. The "magatooth shark" lived in the sea waters above what is now North Carolina, and is estimated to have been 42 feet long, have jaws 6 feet wide and 7 feet high, and teeth 5 inches long. The Museum is preparing an exhibit in which the teeth will be reconstructed to demonstrate the shark jaw, and when visitors push a button, a life-sized image of the rematerialized shark will appear to attack them.

## Ouch, That Smarts

- The most venomous bite on earth is that of the Banded Sea Snake. Divers report that when bitten, victims will experience aching, nausea, spasms, paralysis, and convulsions before dying. They also say the snakes will approach them out of curiosity and curl around their arms and legs.

## Paparazzi Everywhere

- Scientists in Monterey, California, are training sea lions to photograph whales. Equipped with special back harnesses to hold cameras, the sea lions will follow whales in dives of as much as 1,000 feet and provide information not available to human photographers. They are also being training to face the whales continually during the photography sessions, as well as how to "tag" their subjects with special tracking devices mounted on suction cups.

C. WENZEL

## Hang Ten And Then Some

- Legend has it in Hawaii that the highest wave ever ridden was in Waimea Bay in 1868. A fifty-foot tsunami, or tidal wave, barrelled into the beach and surfer "Holua" rode the wave in to save his own life.

- Four to six times a year, the world's longest ridable waves occur on Mtanchen Bay near San Blas, Mexico. Surfers have been verified riding as far as 5,700 feet on one wave.
- The highest tsunami on record, estimated at 278 feet, was off Ishaigaki Island, Japan, on April 24, 1771. While there are no records of any surfers catching that wave, an 830-pound block of coral was thrown 1.3 miles inland by the swell.

## Try Faxing

- Talk about getting nowhere fast. A message in a bottle was recovered on Moreton Island, Queensland, Australia, on June 6, 1983. It has been thrown from the S.S. Arawatta out of Cairns, Queensland, Australia, on June 9, 1910.

# THE LETTER "B"
By Kathy Wolfe

## <u>B</u> Things

- There are about 20,000 different kinds of butterflies. The wingspan of the world's largest butterfly is 11 inches; the smallest is 3/8 of an inch. The butterfly's eyes actually consist of thousands of tiny lenses, with each providing a tiny part of the butterfly's surroundings, which its tiny brain combines into a complete view. The life span of most adult butterflies is only a week or two, although certain kinds live up to 18 months.

- The human brain weighs about 3 lbs. and is divided into two hemispheres, left and right. The functions of language, mathematics, and reasoning appear to be centered in the left, and our abilities in music, expression of emotion, and face recognition are controlled by the right hemisphere.

- The Japanese Samurai have a code of honor which stresses self-discipline, bravery, and simple living. The Japanese word is "Bushido," which means "the way of the warrior."

- The great barracuda lives in the Atlantic Ocean and grows to 6 feet in length. It is an extremely fast fish that is known to attack humans with its razor-sharp teeth. When humans eat the great barracuda, it often leads to a potentially deadly disease called ciguatera.

- The tallest statue in the world, a 1,100-ton likeness of Buddha, is located in Tokyo, Japan, and is 394 feet high. It took seven years to complete. More statues have been built of Buddha than of any other man. Buddha's real name was Siddhartha Gautama, which means "Enlightened One," and he lived around 500 B.C. Buddha preached the message of freeing self from all desires and earthly things. In Buddha's case, this included leaving his wife and newborn son to seek religious enlightenment.

- Barbiturates are used to calm anxiety and help people to sleep by reducing activity within the brain. They were first used in 1903, and phenobarbital, which is used in controlling epileptic seizures, was introduced in 1912. They are extremely addictive and can cause dependence after only four weeks of use. Those withdrawing from their use can expect convulsions, twitching, nightmares, and sleeplessness.

- If botany is your bailiwick, then the study of plant life is your particular area of interest.

- The average life span of a beaver is about 12 years. Beavers have 20 teeth, with the front 4 used for cutting down trees. Some beaver dams are over 1,000 ft. long and more than 12 ft. high. A beaver can hold its breath for 15 minutes.

- Bubonic plague results when a person is bitten by a flea carrying a bacteria from an infected rat. Seventy-five million people died in the "Black Death" plague of 1347-1351. It received the name "Black Death" because the plague produced dark hemorrhages beneath skin and around the eyes, causing the person to die with black, discolored skin. It killed everyone who caught it. It progresses rapidly and the victim can die in less than five days if left untreated. Because it was so incredibly contagious and could be transmitted by a cough or a sneeze, citizens panicked. Parents abandoned sick children, doctors refused to care for the sick, and clergymen refused to pray over the sick. Doctors today can treat the ailment with antibiotics.

- A parakeet with green, yellow, or blue feathers is called a budgerigar, or budgie, for short.
- If you encounter a goblin in the shape of a dog, which is said to warn of coming misfortune, you have seen a barguest. The Old English word "ghest" is their form of our word "ghost".
- The Bronze Star is awarded by the U.S. Army for heroic behavior in ground combat. All ranks of the Armed Forces are eligible to receive it.
- An unusual breed of dogs from Central Africa is the Basenji, which cannot bark; rather, these small dogs make a yodeling sound.

- If you have bradycardia, it means your heart beats fewer than 60 beats per minute (average is 72 to 78). If you are a healthy person who is exercising regularly, this can be normal, but others could be suffering from an underactive thyroid gland or a delay in the beating. Watch for weakness and fainting attacks.
- A blunderbuss with a blunderbuss would be a dangerous combination — a stupid, clumsy person wielding a musket.
- The strongest beer in the world has an alcohol content of

21%. It has the distinctive brand name of "Uncle Igor's Famous Falling Over Water," and is brewed in Great Britain. Beer has been brewed since about 4000 B.C. The oldest brewery in the world is located near Munich, Germany, dating back to the year 1040. The largest brewing company in the world is Anheuser-Busch. Beer is made by mixing barley malt with water and cereal grains. After heating this mixture, the grain is removed and hops are added and boiled again. Yeast is added next, which ferments the sugar into alcohol. The aging process then begins in order to improve the taste. Aging ranges from several weeks to months. The average 12-oz. serving of beer contains 150 calories.

- According to old Irish folklore, the female spirit that warns of an upcoming death in the family by waiting outside the house, is called a banshee.

- If you are an investor in the stock market, you should know that when more people want to sell than buy, the price of stock falls, and the market is called a "bear market." When more people want to buy than sell, stock prices rise, and it is referred to as a "bull market."

- Buttermilk is what remains after cream has been removed from whole milk to make butter. This sour liquid has 2.5 grams of fat per cup, compared to 5 fat grams per cup of 2% milk.

- The black widow spider earned its name from the fact that the female, which is four times larger than the male, kills the male following mating. Although widely believed that its bite causes death in humans, usually only severe pain is the result. The hourglass shape on the underside of its abdomen can be either red or yellow.

## B Folks

- Benjamin Kubelsky was a show business entertainer who began in vaudeville and graduated to motion pictures, radio, and television. His dry sense of humor and accomplished violin playing made him famous. He became known as the man who never aged past 39 (which would have been difficult, considering he was married for over 47 years). Of course, he is better known as Jack Benny.

- In 1954, Roger Bannister became the first man to run a mile in less than four minutes — 3 minutes, 59.4 seconds, to be exact. It took only a month for this record to be broken by another runner. Two months later, Bannister once again broke the record.

- Anne Boleyn was the second of the six wives of King Henry VIII. She was the maid of honor at the wedding of the first wife, and Henry became interested in her at that time. Although she bore him a daughter, who went on to rule England for 45 years as Elizabeth, after 3 years of marriage, she had failed to produce a male heir. The king made the decision to have her beheaded and trumped up charges of adultery and plotting to kill the king, which carried the death penalty. Anne was flippant about her sentence, saying, "The executioner is very good. I have a little neck."

- The original name of the Beach Boys was Carl & the Passions. With all their numerous hit records, they have never won a Grammy. Leonard Bernstein, on the other hand, won 16 Grammy Awards.

- Scottish-born Alexander Graham Bell (a talented musician and a teacher of the deaf) attended school for only five years and was educated almost entirely at home. When tuberculosis threatened his health, he moved to North America. Six years later, he received a patent for the first telephone.

- Work began on Mt. Rushmore in the Black Hills of South Dakota in 1927. Its sculptor was Gurzon Borglum, who studied in Paris but was born in Idaho.

- Ludwig van Beethoven wrote much of his most famous music after he was totally deaf. His hearing loss began at age 31 and progressed to total deafness at age 49. This genius suffered from smallpox as a child, and as an adult from asthma, migraines, pancreatitis, irritable bowel syndrome, depressions, and what is thought to have been lupus, finally succumbing to cirrhosis of the liver. Not surprisingly, he often contemplated suicide. Over 20,000 attended his funeral. Thirty years after his death, his body was exhumed and his ear bones were studied before he was reburied.

- The voice of Mr. Magoo and the man who played millionaire Thurston Howell III on TV's "Gilligan's Island" were both Jim Backus.

- Louis Braille was 15 years old when, as a student at an institution for the blind, he developed a reading system for the blind consisting of raised dots felt with the fingertips. He went on to teach his fellow blind as well as to become a church organist.

- The woman who penned the words to "America the Beautiful" was Katherine Bates, who did so while standing at the top of Pikes Peak.

- The Beatles first called themselves by that name in 1960 as a tribute to Buddy Holly, leader of the musical group The Crickets, who had been killed in a tragic plane crash in 1959. Prior to using the name The Beatles, they had performed under several names, including The Quarreymen, Johnny & The Moondogs, and The Moonshiners. Ringo Starr was not one of the original Beatles, and did not join them until 1962, replacing drummer Pete Best. Their premiere on the Ed Sullivan Show was on Feb. 9, 1964. They remained together until 1970.

- In 1881, President James Garfield was shot by an assassin at the Washington, D.C., railroad depot. Dr. Willard Bliss was the first doctor to examine the injured Garfield. He stuck both an unwashed finger and a contaminated metal instrument deep into his wound, searching for the bullet that was causing blood poisoning. Dr. Bliss was unsuccessful in finding the bullet, but did manage, along with several other doctors with unsterile hands, to introduce several infections into Garfield's body, which, along with the bullet's poisoning, were the cause of Garfield's death.

- It was not Walt Disney who created Peter Pan but Sir James Barrie, a Scottish novelist who, in 1904, wrote the play about the boy who refused to grow up.
- Mel Blanc was the voice of Bugs Bunny, Porky Pig, Sylvester the Cat, Tweetie Bird, and countless other cartoon characters. The first time Bugs uttered his trademark "What's up, doc?" was in his fifth film, "A Wild Hare," in 1939.
- The suits and sunglasses worn by John Belushi and Dan Ackroyd in the movie "The Blues Brothers" were sold at an auction for $12,000.
- Their real names: Tony Bennett — Antonio Dominick Benedetto; Charles Bronson — Charles Buchinsky; Richard Burton — Richard Jenkins; Birdman of Alcatraz — Robert Stroud; Batman — Bruce Wayne; Blondie — Mrs. Dagwood Bumstead; Marlon Brando — Marlon Brando.

## B Places

- The world's first steel-wire suspension bridge was the Brooklyn Bridge, which connects Brooklyn and Manhattan. It was built at a cost of $15 million back in 1883. A suspension bridge has a road that hangs from steel cables that are supported by two high towers. The cables of the Brooklyn Bridge are 16 inches thick.
- If Brooklyn were classfied as an independent city, rather than a borough of New York City, it would rank as the fourth largest city in the U.S. It was incorporated as a city in 1834, although Dutch settlers had inhabited the area since the 1600's.
- Travel 16 miles north of Buffalo, New York, and you will reach Niagara Falls, which is responsible for Buffalo's low-cost hydroelectric power rates. This city is the largest producer of flour in the U.S.
- Death toll at Germany's Nazi concentration camp Buchenwald is estimated at 57,000. Death came by murder, starvation, disease, or being worked to death. Some were killed by being used as guinea pigs for "scientific medical experiments." It was not unusual for a prisoner to lose 50%

of his body weight while interned in a concentration camp. All remaining prisoners were liberated by U.S. forces in April, 1945.

- Father Flanagan's Boys' Home is located near Omaha, Nebraska, and is more commonly known as Boys' Town. Flanagan was a Catholic priest who established the home in 1917 to house the homeless, abused, and disabled. An old Omaha house, home for five boys, began with $90 in borrowed rent money and grew to a 160-acre farm, and today covers 1,300 acres.

## Quotes To Note

- "If only I were rid of my affliction, I would embrace the whole world." –Beethoven
- "O God, have pity on my soul. O God, have pity on my soul ..." –last words of Anne Boleyn
- "Never forget it: decay is inherent in all things." –Buddha
- "There is no such thing as a bad boy." –Boys Town motto
- "Never have more children than you have car windows. Never loan your car to someone to whom you have given birth."

    –Erma Bombeck

- "If a man measures life by what others do for him, he is apt to be disappointed; but if he measures life by what he does for others, there is no time for despair." –William Jennings Bryan, three-time unsuccessful candidate for President

# PIRATES AND THEIR TREASURE
By Mona McKown

- Definition: 1. one who commits or practices piracy: as a) a robber on the high seas b) one noted for predatory practices/ financial c) an infringer of the law of copyright.
- Pirates were also called buccaneers, corsairs, filibusters, freebooters, ladrones, pickaroons, and sea rovers.
- Piracy was most prevalent from the 1500's through the 1700's on the Mediterranean and Caribbean seas.
- The most famous pirates were Henry Morgan, Blackbeard, and William Kidd.
- People became pirates for various reasons. Sometimes, honest seamen would desert or mutiny their ships because of the harsh conditions at sea, after which they would turn to piracy to survive.
- Legend, fiction, and motion pictures have helped create an exciting and romantic image of pirates. However, in real life, most pirates led miserable lives. They were generally quarrelsome and often drunk. Many died from disease or wounds. Some pirates were even shot or marooned by their own crews.
- Pirate ships flew a red banner called the Bloody Flag until about 1700. After that they began using flags with pictures of various objects such as skeletons, flaming swords, and hourglasses. The most popular flag was the Jolly Roger which showed a white skull and crossbones on a black background.

## Pirates Of The Mediterranean

- Piracy on the Mediterranean resulted from a rivalry between Muslims and Christians. Muslim pirates from the Barbary States, which were along the coast of northern Africa, sailed the Mediterranean and attacked the ships of France, Italy, Spain, and other Christian nations of Europe. The Barbary corsairs, as they were called, had bases in Algiers, Tunis, and Tripoli. The most famous leaders of the Barbary corsairs were Occhiali, Arouj, and Khair-ed-Din Barbarossa, who were brothers, Dragut, Ali Pasha, and a woman, Jeanne de Belleville.

## American Pirates

- Captain Nathaniel Gordon was the last American pirate to be hanged. In the mid-19th Century the smuggling of slaves was the chief trade of American pirates. On Gordon's fourth voyage, he was captured by the American ship Mohican. He was aboard the 500-ton Erie and below its decks were 967 blacks. Three hundred of those had died on the journey from Africa because of such poor conditions. Gordon was charged with piracy, stood trial in New York, and was found guilty, after which he was sentenced to death. Many protested, claiming it was unjust to execute a man for a crime that had been virtually extinct for 40 years. A petition for pardon was submitted to President Lincoln, but the death sentence was upheld. On March 8, 1862, Nathaniel Gordon was hanged in "the Tombs" in New York City.
- Stede Bonnet, a retired army major, took up piracy in 1717, but was caught and hanged within a year's time.
- The gentleman pirate, Bartholomew Roberts, didn't allow drinking or gambling on his ship, and he never fought on Sunday. He captured more ships than any other Atlantic pirate.
- Ned Low was a madman who was so cruel that his own crew set him adrift in an open boat without food, water or weapons. He was picked up by a passing boat and taken to the island of Martinique where he was hanged.
- The first pirate on the Atlantic seaboard was Dixie Bull in

1632. He became a pirate to avenge himself because his shallop was seized by a French pinnace and his goods were taken.

## Blackbeard

- The ferocious British pirate, Edward Teach, had a pigtailed beard, which gave him the name "Blackbeard." He stood six-feet-four-inches and weighed 250 pounds. He wore six pistols strapped to his chest and could handle a 10-pound cutlass as if it were a dueling sword. He also had fourteen wives and is supposed to have buried treasure in hundreds of places.

- The Isles of Shoals are a group of islands off the coast of New Hampshire. Blackbeard used to rendezvous on these islands with his other pirate captains. One story about these rendezvouses tells of Sandy Gordon, a captain of the Flying Scot and a Blackbeard confederate, splitting the treasure taken from a Spanish galleon. Gordon then buried his share on White Island and left his girlfriend, Martha, to guard it. Soon after, Sandy Gordon was killed in a battle with a British warship.

- Blackbeard built a house on Plum Point in Beaufort County, North Carolina. In 1716, he and his men were seen burying an iron chest in a low sandy place not far from the house. The legend of the chest has caused many to dig for the buried treasure. In 1928, two trappers found a large hole near a very old tree. This hole contained an empty vault made of old- fashioned bricks. The chest had left impressions in the mortar, and grooves made by the straps that held the chest shut, could clearly be seem. But the chest was gone and no one knows who actually dug it up.

- Blackbeard literally lost his head in a sea battle near Ocracoke Island, off North Carolina, in 1718. It is believed that the largest part of Blackbeard's treasure may still be buried there, as the island was his headquarters at that time.

## Jean Lafitte

- Jean Lafitte, a French pirate, and his men took millions in loot from ships in the Gulf of Mexico in the early 1800's. It is believed that he buried most of his treasure somewhere around New Orleans, Louisiana, or Galveston, Texas.

- Jean Lafitte was already a rich man when he settled in New Orleans, but he continued his smuggling activities, using a blacksmith shop as a front. Lafitte quickly became the leader of the local pirates, but after the authorities put so much pressure on him for his illegal activities, he moved to Galveston Island, which was under Spanish control. On Galveston Island he collected a 20% rake-off on all the treasure taken by about 1,000 of the local pirates. When he was driven from the island, it is believed he had more than $10 million, which he took aboard his ship the Pride.

- Supposedly, the Pride ran aground on a sandbar near the mouth of the Laraca River, which is not far from Corpus Christi, Texas. Lafitte was to have buried his $10 million on land nearby, later owned by a rancher named Hill. Lafitte marked the spot with a jacob staff, a brass rod used to support a compass. The treasure has never been found but many have searched.

- In 1920, a fisherman brought up three silver bars from Hendrick's Lake, near Galveston, Texas. Hendrick's Lake is where Lafitte supposedly dumped $2 million in silver ingots which were taken from the Spanish brig, the *Santa Rosa*.

- Lafitte also had a brother who was a notorious pirate. His name was Pierre. Together, they established themselves in

Barataria Bay in New Orleans. The Lafittes plundered in the Gulf of Mexico and various other bays. They preyed on Spanish shipping and on slavers that supplied the West Indian plantations. The slaves that they captured were sold to the Louisiana planters for a dollar a pound. The Lafitte brothers continued piracy and were arrested by the governor but were acquitted after being defended by the best legal aid available. Pierre disappeared and no one really knows what happened to him.

## Treasures Found And Lost

- Just before the Civil War, John Singer found a chest containing $80,000 worth of gold and jewels on Padre Island. Lafitte had supposedly buried some of his treasure on the island. Unfortunately, John Singer reburied the uncovered treasure for safekeeping during the Civil War, and was never able to relocate it afterwards.

- Four hundred miles off Costa Rica on the Pacific Ocean side, lies the Cocos Island. Many treasures were supposedly buried on the island at the end of the 17th Century. The most famous of these treasures is the Lima treasure. It is reputedly worth over $20 million. In 1823, a group of Spaniards in Lima "liberated" the Peruvian state treasure. It consisted partially of 113 gold religious statues, 200 chests of jewels, 250 jeweled swords, 150 chalices, 300 bars of gold, and 600 bars of silver. A bishop, the governor of Lima, and some other Spaniards went aboard the *Mary Dier*, under the command of William Thompson, to help keep watch over the vast treasure. Captain Thompson and his crew became greedy and killed the bishop and the others. Now a pirate, Thompson sailed to Cocos Island where he stashed the treasure in a cave. As his ship left the island it was attacked and captured by the Spanish frigate, *Espiegle*. Under duress, Captain Thompson and a crew member were taken to the island to find the treasure. Thompson, however, escaped and hid. After searching in vain for the treasure and Thompson, the *Espiegle* sailed off.

A month later, a whaler anchored and the crew came ashore for a fresh supply of water. There they found Thompson, who said his companion had died. Thompson never was able to return to the island, but did give his friend, John Keating, a chart and detailed information about where the treasure was hidden. The story continues with Keating and a companion going to Cocos Island to look for the hidden treasure. They did not tell the ship's crew what they had in mind, but it wasn't very long until they figured it out. The crew mutinied. The two men escaped from the ship to the island and hid. Keating, like Thompson, was rescued by a whaler and reported that his companion had died, too. Keating also failed to return to the island and passed his secret to a friend. Several attempts, involving hundreds of people, between the years of 1872 to 1932, were made to try to locate the lost treasures of Cocos Island with only minimal findings.

## William Kidd

- Captain William Kidd was one of the most famous pirates although he practiced piracy only for a brief time. He was stereotyped as a hang-'em-from-the-yardarms pirate because of the exaggerations of his crimes by British government officials. He allegedly buried his treasures in several places.
- In 1699, Captain William Kidd was sailing in the Caribbean, when he heard that he had been declared an outlaw. After hearing the news, he went to Gardiners Island, which is off New York's Long Island, to bury the treasure he had on board his ship. After hiding his treasure of gold and jewels, which was worth more than $50,000, he began negotiating for his life with the governor of New York, Lord Bellamont. His negotiations failed, however, and Kidd was hanged. Part of the treasure was recovered but part still remains buried, possibly in a swampy section of the island.

## Treasured Quotes

- "There is nothing so desperately monotonous as the sea, and I no longer wonder at the cruelty of pirates." – James Russell Lowell

- "It is, it is a glorious thing, To be a Pirate King"

  –Sir William Gilbert
- "There was no getting around the stubborn fact that taking sweetmeats was only 'hooking,' while taking bacon and hams and such valuables was plain simple stealing – and there was a command against that in the Bible. So they inwardly resolved that so long as they remained in the business, their piracies should not again be sullied with the crime of stealing."

  – Mark Twain
- "It is when pirates count their booty that they become mere thieves." –William Bolitho
- "When a Pirate prays, there is great danger." – Thomas Fuller

## A Caribbean Pirate

- In the late 18th and early 19th Centuries Jose Gaspar, known as Gasparilla, operated in the Caribbean as a pirate. He made his base on Gasparilla Island on the Gulf coast of Florida. When he captured the American cargo ship Orleans in September, 1821, he took off $40,000 worth of cargo. In 1822, Gasparilla and his men attacked what they thought to be an unarmed merchant man. It, however, proved to be a U. S. warship in disguise. When his ship was about to be captured and he realized execution was in store for him, Gasparilla wrapped a heavy anchor chain around his waist, jumped overboard, and drowned.

## The Last Look

- Anne Bonny was an illegitimate Irish child. Her father was a prominent lawyer, William Cormac, and her mother was Peg Brennan, the family maid. Because of the scandal, Cormac moved his little family to Charleston, South Carolina, where he started a merchant business and became quite wealthy. Anne had a violent temper and, though the stories were exaggerated, she did stab a servant girl with a table knife and beat up a young suitor when she was 13 years of age. Anne eventually married a penniless man named James Bonny. Anne soon grew to dislike her husband and turned her affections to a young pirate named Calico Jack Rackam. Rackam tried to purchase Anne, as divorce by sale was common. However, Bonny refused the offer and reported the liason to Governor Woods Rogers, who was trying to clean out all the pirates. The Governor threatened to have Anne flogged if she did not return to her husband. Anne and Rackam decided to run away and go pirating together.

# LESSOR KNOWN FACTS

By V.B. Darrington

- Your birth order may be your birthright. For example, if you are an only child, you have a statistically better chance of having a high IQ than people who grow up with siblings. Unfortunately, without the benefit of a built-in "support group," you may suffer loneliness or isolation in some aspects of your life.
- First-born children complain about having to bear all the responsibilities, while their younger siblings get off easy. On the bright side, oldest children enjoy more parental attention than younger kids, and they become adept at taking care of other people.
- Middle children seem to get less attention than those born at the beginning or end. But they adapt by becoming capable at manipulating situations. They are good at getting along with other people and compromising.
- Youngest children are stuck with wearing hand-me-downs. They get treated like children far longer than they might appreciate. But on the bright side, they also get a lot of attention, as well as live-in tutors in the form of older siblings.
- Ancient Egyptians believed that children could see into the future.
- In 1212, some 30,000 children voluntarily left their homes, to follow a 12-year-old shepherd boy named Stephen. In what became known as the Children's Crusade, the children marched after their young leader in order to join the great

war to help free the Holy Land from the Saracens.
- The children converged on the French port of Marseilles. There, they were offered passage to the Middle East by two merchant ship owners, Hugh the Iron and William the Pig. Tragically, before reaching the battle field, the children were kidnapped, sold in Algeria, and forced into a life of slavery.
- In the 1600's, boys wore dresses until the age of 6 or 7. Then, they were "breached," taken and fitted with trousers. Little girls of the same time period wore corsets of steel or whalebone. The garments were so tight that the girls could not bend over.
- In the late 1800's, more than 100,000 orphans joined the "Orphan Train." The orphans were gathered from urban areas in the East and shipped by train to the New Frontier. Settler families in the West would meet the Orphan Train and review the candidates for adoption. The orphans would stand in line wearing a tag telling their age and name. If a family found a suitable child, they would be able to adopt him or her before the train left the station. The adopted children were an important source of labor for the struggling, young frontier families.
- William James Sidis was a child prodigy, but not by choice. His father contended that a child could be taught to learn much quicker than was customarily accepted. He pushed his son relentlessly. By age 4, William could type in English and in French. He entered first grade on a normal schedule, but he quickly covered 7 years' of course work in 6 months. Young Sidis was educationally qualified for college at the age of 9, but Harvard declined to accept him until he was 11.
- When William reached his 11th birthday, he became Harvard's youngest student. He was instantly famous for his understanding of physics and mathematics. And he was occasionally called upon to lecture on the topics. Only a year later, William broke down. The pressure of being an academic anomaly seemed too intense for the young boy. His parents

sent him away to rest, and he eventually recovered sufficiently to return to college. Back at school, Sidis was not the same.

- He became a loner, refusing to bathe regularly, and rejecting social companionship. William cultured a strong hatred for his father. Finally, when his father died, the young genius commented that he didn't want to hear about it. Sidis ended up working as a clerk and died alone at the age of 46.

- George Bidder was a child sensation. He could figure seemingly impossible mathematic calculations without the use of paper or pencil. While still a child, he taught himself multiplication by arranging small pieces of lead shot into tables and graphs. His father quickly capitalized on the boy's talent and took him on tour.

- At one show, when George was 11, he was read a 43-digit number. Then, he was asked to repeat the number in reverse order. He did so without problem. For another hour George was questioned about unrelated math topics. Out of the blue, a spectator asked him if he could still repeat the 43-digit number in reverse and forward order. George did. On another occasion, a heckler in the crowds asked George how many bulls' tails it would take to reach the

moon. George replied quickly, "One, if it's long enough."

- After watching his father play just four games of chess, Jose Capablanca noticed that the Knight moved in an odd pattern. He pointed this out to his father, who whimsically challenged the 4-year-old to a match. Jose surprised his father, winning two games in a row. Jose's parents recognized the boy's miraculous talent. But, they did not allow him to play much chess until he was eight. They had been advised by a doctor that the mental strain might be bad for the young prodigy. Finally, when Jose was 12, he enter the chess world. He defeated his country's reigning chess champion to become the Cuban national champion. A few years later, at 20, Jose traveled to the US. In 734 games, he won 703.

- In 1921, Capablanca became the World Champion and traveled extensively. The great champion seldom studied tactics or moves from books or other players. Instead, he played by instinct. He was known for his wonderful end-game maneuvers. Aptly, Jose Capablanca was nicknamed the "Chess Machine."

## Sports Nuts

- Baseball, the American pastime, has its roots in Great Britain. A British game called "rounders" was brought to America only in relatively recent history.

- The British game became known as "town ball." The game used heavy stones or wooden stakes for bases. The pitcher was known then as a "feeder" or "pecker." Hitters ran the bases clockwise, or the reverse of what players run today. After hitting the ball, runners would attempt to round the bases, while the defense would attempt to "plug" the runner by hitting him with the ball.

- In 1845, a group of health-conscious gentlemen in New York decided to adapt the game to their needs. They invented some of the baseball conventions that we still have today. Teams had nine players, the field became diamond-shaped, and the bases were changed to flat bags. By the new rules, a team was declared the winner not after nine innings, but when the first team scored 21 runs. In order to control the rowdy play, the men's club established monetary fines for rule infractions. Arguing with an umpire cost 25 cents; swearing, 6 cents.

- Although Hank Aaron is known as the home-run king in the U.S., another person holds the all-time home-run world record. A man named Sadaharu Oh hit nearly one hundred more dingers than Aaron. Sadaharu played for the Yomiuri Giants in the Japanese professional leagues. But give "Hammerin' Hank" his due respect. Japanese parks are considerably smaller than North American playing fields.

## Hoopball

- A Canadian transplant invented the great American sport of basketball. James Naismith thought up the game in an attempt to keep athletes in shape during the cold winter months.

- The first basketball game had little in common with our current pastime. Instead of a hoop, a peach basket was nailed onto a gymnasium balcony. Players used a soccer ball and wore body pads much like football players do.

- Basketball courts did not have standard dimensions. So, players used walls as boundaries, with radiators and doorways all a part of the playing field. When a ball went out of bounds, the first player to touch the ball got to throw it in. As a result, players frequently charged into spectators, and even down flights of stairs in an attempt to get the ball first. At one point, fences were added to the court sides in an effort to keep balls from going out of bounds.

- The early fans of basketball were a rough-and-ready crowd. Fans would tussle with players as they attempted to get out-of-bounds balls. In Pennsylvania, particularly, the fans went berserk. Local coal miners would come to the game armed with nails and mining helmets. They would heat the nails in the flame of the lantern, and throw the red-hot projectiles at the referee and the players. Some fans were known to bring hairpins to the game, to impale any player who might get near enough.

## Bowling

- Bowling is one of the oldest sports of all times. Historians estimate that people have been playing versions of the game for over 7,000 years. A bowling set was found even in the tomb of an Egyptian boy.

- Modern bowling came to us from Germany. There, they

played the sport in churches. The pins represented the devil, and the ball was used to strike him down. Martin Luther was a big fan of the sport. He personally invented a version of bowling called "ninepins."

- In the 1930's, ninepins became very popular in the U.S. Regrettably, when organized gambling took an interest in the sport, it was outlawed in many areas. The game of "tenpins" was invented to end-run the restrictive laws.

- Today, over 40 million Americans enjoy the sport. In this decade, a huge facility has been built in Reno, Nevada, a sort of bowling "Mecca." At the new multi-floored facility, bowlers can choose from a variety of pro shops and bowling venues. A bowler can get computer analysis of his form, or can have his game videotaped for later reference.

## Boxing

- The first recorded history of boxing comes to us from Greece, about three thousand years ago. Greek contestants wrapped their hands in leather strips and fought until exhausted. The winner was rewarded with a mule; the loser, a drinking cup.

- Romans soon adopted the sport. They obligated prisoners to be the contestants in huge boxing extravaganzas. Roman fighters used leather hand wraps, but they also added metal spikes and hand weights. Many of the fights were to the death.

- On the civilized island of Great Britain, contestants fought in gruesome bare-handed duels that allowed gouging, hair-pulling, and wrestling. When a fighter was knocked down, his supporters would pull him from the ring and revive him with draughts of whiskey. Fights seemed to last forever.

- Our version of modern prize fighting was born in England. In the late 1800's, two Englishmen wrote rules for the sport. Rounds were limited to three minutes, no gouging or holding was allowed, and fighters were required to wear padded gloves.

## On The Ice

- Figure skating is an American invention. A ballet teacher named Jackson Haines moved to Europe at about the time of the Civil War in hopes of improving his lagging business. Jackson Haines discovered ice skating while in the Netherlands and combined it with his beloved ballet. The American dancer dazzled the staid Europeans by jumping and spinning on the ice, while wearing bold, colorful costumes.

- Indeed, skating has come a long way in the past 2,000 years. In the earliest days, skates were made of bones and wood. Skating was a practical affair, a way to get around town in the Netherlands when the canals had frozen in winter. Early skaters usually skated while standing upright, their hands crossed on their chest to keep them warm.

- As equipment and skating venues have improved, the sport has exploded in Europe and in the U.S. Today there are more than 2,000 indoor skating rinks in the U.S., and more than 20,000,000 skaters.

## The Final Fact

- In the highest-scoring game in football history, in 1916, Georgia Tech outscored Cumberland College 222-0.

# FASHION
By J.C. Walker

## Bring On The Leisure Suits

- Fashion mavens tell us the hot new trend for this season is the "safari look," which has also been dubbed "the hippie-adventuress look." For those of you with no imagination, this must-have list includes suede flare pants (aka: bellbottoms), animal prints, and khaki bush jackets outfitted with lariat neckties. Imagine the stir in the office when you walk in in your V-neck laced shirt, vinyl faux crocodile hip hugger pants, and python print jacket trimmed in dyed monkey fur. A look to die for.

## Sock It To Me

- Over 80,000 people have already visited the year-old Bata Shoe Museum in Toronto. They have oohed and ahhed over Queen Victoria's slippers, samuri shoes, Indian snow boots, Elvis' blue and white loafers, peasant clogs with spikes for crushing chestnuts, and boots Winston Churchill wore during WWII, among other things. The collection was put together by Sonia Bata, wife of a European shoe tycoon, during the 50 years of their marriage, and is far larger than could all be put on display at any one time. The latest acquisition is a pair of socks worn by Napoleon during his exile on St. Helena, for which the museum shelled out $4,400 at a Sotheby's auction. Also remarkable are the items not on view – museum staff have not yet acquired a sample from Imelda Marcos, the Philippines' Queen of Soles, who owns an estimated 30,000 pairs of shoes. But they're working on it.

## Jeans Therapy

- Jeans continue to enjoy enormous popularity in the United States and abroad. Vintage jeans are also an investment. For $2,500, a Denver couple bought from a retired Levi Strauss salesman, a pair of unworn jeans made in 1927. He'd paid $3.02 in the early 50's. They recently refused a $30,000 offer from a Japanese jeans fan, the couple believes they'll eventually get $75,000 for their trouble.

- Jeans really were invented by Levi Strauss. He'd heard California gold miners complain that plain cotton work pants couldn't hold up in the rigors of panning and pawing, so he took a French fabric called denim and sewed up some britches with double stitching and rivets. "Levis" were born in the year of the gold rush of 1849, and it's believed the famous 501 style got its name from a pre-1906 wholesale catalog that used that number to identify a new waist-high overall design.

- A recent charity art auction for a children's hospital in Australia tried a new twist. Celebrities such as Monica Seles, Richard Harris, Candice Bergen, Robin Williams, Luciano Pavarotti and Julio Iglesias donated their well-worn jeans. Famous local artists used them as the canvases for their individual and often outrageous artistic expression. Donors paid major bucks for ragged  workpants covered with paint to hang on their walls, but all for a good cause called Jeans for Genes.

## Still Doing It

- The latest shoe craze in Japan is early design athletic shoes from Nike, Adidas, Converse, and Puma. Schoolkids are paying as much as $80 for a pair of slightly used 1982 Nikes, and one collector recently paid $1,000 for a pair of never-worn, 1985 Nike Dunks. Prices for other highly valued models range from $100 to $500. Observers recognize that the shoes are not coveted for their use in sports, but for status, since Japanese children and teenagers must wear school uniforms, and the recycled status symbols are one of the few ways wearers can set themselves apart.

## Not Greasy Kid Stuff

- Hair pomade in a variety of colors is the rage in New York salons. Sold in shoe polish tins, the pomade gives hair the shining tints of blue, gold, silver, black, brown, or bordeaux.

## We Are Not Alone In The Closet, Either

- Alien abductees and their supporters can advertise their experiences non-verbally by wearing a new fashion line called Invasion Clothing. T-shirts and sweatshirts are imprinted with non-fading, glow-in-the-dark prints, and the designs have names like UFO V2.0, Spaceman, Saturn, Spidey, Trihead, Alien Ovum, Saturn Sweatshirt, Sprawl, and The Webmaster.

## Clothes Quotes

- "On the fourth day of telecommuting, I realized that clothes are totally unnecessary." – Dilbert
- "I come from a country where you don't wear clothes most of the year. Nudity is the most natural state. I was born nude and I hope to be buried nude. – Elle MacPherson, Australian model and actress
- "To reduce the accumulation of static electricity, you must increase the humidity, change or get rid of the carpeting, or both. Although a small room-sized humidifier may help, these steps are often too expensive to be practical. A less expensive step is to avoid wearing leather soled shoes or clothes made of synthetic fibers. (If possible, compute in the nude.) Weather (sic) or not you take any of these steps, you should still touch metal to dissipate the static charge before you touch the computer or a disk." – From the book *Supercharging MS-Dos* by Microsoft Press, in the section, *"Static Electricity is a Killer"*

- "Beware of all enterprises that require new clothes."
  – Henry David Thoreau
- "Clothes therefore, must be truly a badge of greatness; the insignia of the superiority of man over all other animals, for surely there could be no other reason for wearing the hideous things." – Tarzan
- "Take off all your clothes and walk down the street waving a machete and firing an Uzi, and terrified citizens will phone the police and report: 'There's a naked person outside!'"
  – Mike Nichols

## No Surprise Atoll

- The Bikini bathing suit celebrates its fiftieth birthday this year. First modeled in a Paris fashion show in 1946, the style was considered scandalous since the wearer's navel was exposed. The style was promoted by saavy advertisers who used skywriting campaigns over French Riviera beaches to promote the message: "Bikini – smaller than the smallest bathing suit in the world." It took about twenty years for the idea really to catch on, and now the "dental floss thong" is the Bikini of choice. Bikinis outsell one-piece suits three to two.

## Bits And Pieces

- Small babies in Africa wear sun bonnets made from gourds cut in half and carved with elaborate symbols.
- The Glen Eden 1st Annual Chili Cook-Off was a huge success this past summer. It was the first clothing optional event of its kind in Corona, California, and from the 800 who were invited, 30 well-known chili chefs attended. The facility provided full-length bib aprons.
- Throw out that sunscreen – medical scientists have developed UV-blocking clothes and hats with an SPF of as much as 30.
- Venezuela is always well represented in international beauty pagents. It's true the country is known for beautiful women, but it also has a center devoted entirely to preparing contestants. They spend up to three months at a time in quarantine in the facility where they are massaged, dieted,

aerobicized, and quizzed with beauty pagent questions in preparation for the next event.

- The Codpiece Restoration Society is a branch of an international organization dedicated to the popular revival of this article of men's clothing worn in the 14th, 15th, and 16th centuries. The codpiece has nothing to do with fish.

## Made In The Shades

- In the early 1900's fashion was dictated by the new invention taking the country by storm. Whole new businesses and catalogs were completely devoted to outfitting the "automobilist" properly. Without enclosed cabs on the new horseless carriages, a 50 MPH spin in the country could be a chilling experience even in the middle of summer, so people wore massive leather and fur masks, blankets, gauntlet gloves, dusters, and hats. The great-great grandaddy of sunglasses also came out of this era – women carried special fans that enclosed two transparent celluloid panels, one clear and the other smoked, to protect their eyes from glare and flying debris.

## Don't Forget The Rogaine

- First it was tail-fins, then it was Motown. Detroit now can boast it's the birthplace of the zippered hairdo. At a recent hair fashion show, the creator of the new look brought out a model with a two-and-a-half-foot high French twist at the back of her head, the style secured by a giant zipper. As the hair stylist turned her away from the audience, he unzipped her hair and pulled out a live, four-foot python. There are reports that in previous shows he has produced live doves and a bottle of champagne with two glasses from the model's tresses.

## Corsets True

- Madonna isn't the only dancer in history to have pranced around in her underwear. Archeologists have discovered Minoan wall paintings on the island of Crete which feature a dancer wearing nothing but a corset and a sweet smile.

# What's In A Name

- The expression "the cat's pajamas" means something is the best or the ultimate in status. It began in the mid-1800's when London aristocracy flocked in droves to a shop known for its high quality Chinese silk pajamas. The shop was owned by Mr. Katz.

# Support Group

- The invention of the bra was a complicated matter. The original bra-type device was put together by a garment worker named Otto Titzling (really) in 1912 for a singer who resided in the same boarding house. Otto saw he was on to a good thing as the woman, Swanhilda Olafsen (really) carried a substantial feminine frame and required a little structural support to reach those high notes. He then went on to invent undergarments for the less well-endowed and even an inflatable bra. His idea was brazenly stolen by a French designer named Phillipe de Brassiere (really) who had a better eye for feminine frillery that was more marketable, and he went on to cash in on the trend as women began to dress more simply and comfortably. Sadly, Otto had not bothered to patent his original 1912 design, although he'd done so with later pieces, and lost his lawsuit against the designer. The trial made headlines for weeks as Titzling and Brassiere used beautiful young models to present the different designs during the proceedings. When it all ended in 1938, the word "bra" appeared in the Dictionary of American Slang for the first time.

# And You Thought Fashion Was Dumb

- Professional models offer career tips and reassurance that civilization as we know it will continue:
- Barbi Benton: "I believe that mink are raised for being turned into fur coats and if we didn't wear fur coats those little animals would never have been born. So is it better not to have been born or to have lived for a year or two to have been turned into a fur coat? I don't know."

- Cindy Crawford: "They were doing a full back shot of me in a swimsuit and I thought, Oh my God, I have to be so brave. See, every woman hates herself from behind."
- Christie Brinkley: "I wish my butt did not go sideways, but I guess I have to face that."
- Linda Evangelista: "I can do anything you want me to do so long as I don't have to speak."
- Carole Mallory: "Everywhere I went, my cleavage followed. But I learned I am not my cleavage."
- Paulina Porizkova: "When I model I'm pretty blank. You can't think too much or it doesn't work."
- Cheryl Tiegs: "It's very important to have the right clothing to exercise in. If you throw on an old T-shirt or sweats, it's not inspiring for your workout."
- Veronica Webb: "When my Azzedine jacket from 1987 died, I wrapped it up in a box, attached a note saying where it came from and took it to the Salvation Army. It was a big loss."

# LEGENDS OF THE WILD WEST

by Kathy Wolfe

## Wild Bill Hickok

- James Butler Hickok was known as "Duck Bill" before he was "Wild Bill," because of his long nose and upper lip, which stuck out. It was his expert marksman skills which earned him the name "Wild Bill," Before becoming the legendary sheriff of Abilene, Kansas, he was a farmworker, stagecoach driver, wagonmaster, Civil War Union spy, and scout for Custer's Seventh Cavalry. With two six-guns in his belt, he was considered the best gunman in Kansas Territory.

- Wild Bill was 6'2", with long hair flowing past his shoulders, often formed into ringlets held in place with hair oil. This fancy dresser, with suits with satin lapels, colorful silk ties, flower-lined cape, checkered pants, and even a corset, was a deadly gunfighter before his lawman days. Whenever any of his shoot-outs were investigated, they were labeled "justifiable."

- When Abilene became a thriving cow town as the result of Texas cattle drives, Hickok was appointed sheriff, earning $150 a month for his services. He supplemented his income as a regular at the gambling tables of the Alamo Saloon. Wild Bill could not be called Abilene's most honest sheriff, preferring to accept bribe money from gamblers and pimps rather than interfere in their business.

- Bill was sheriff just shy of 7 months, being relieved of his position when he killed two innocent men (including his own deputy who had come to his aid), after being interrupted from the gambling tables. Being hard up for cash, he joined a Wild West show, but found the work "tiring and degrading." But evidence points to the beginnings of blindness. Medical reports showed "advanced glaucoma in left eye and would soon be completely blind." Five months before his death, he remarked to an acquaintance, "My shooting days are over. The best I can do now is to see a man's form indistinctly at sixteen paces."

- About that time, Wild Bill married Agnes Lake Thatcher, whom he had rescued from the jaws of a lion in a Wild West show. She was not with him in Deadwood, South Dakota, at the time of his death. He had written a letter to her a mere 24 hours before his death, stating that he would "gently breathe" her name while firing his last shot, as if he had a premonition of his own death.

- It was in August of 1876 that Hickok was in the midst of a draw poker game when Jack McCall, who claimed that Hickok had killed his brother, placed a bullet in the back of Bill's head. McCall claimed that when he was 12 years old and his brother was 9, the younger boy had called Hickok "Duck Bill," a name Bill despised. Hickok allegedly flew into a rage, grabbed a hoe, and struck the boy a fatal blow to the head. Jack vowed at that moment, "I'll kill you when I grow up!"

- With his gunslinger's instincts to the end, Wild Bill had his right-hand gun half out of its holster when his face hit the poker table. In his other hand, he clutched his cards, which showed two pairs, Aces and 8's, which thereafter became known as "the dead man's hand."

- McCall's trial began the next day. By evening a verdict of not guilty was returned and McCall was a free man for nearly 4 months. At that time his verdict was thrown out, claiming that trial was held in a court which was not considered legal. The new trial lasted several days, and this time a guilty verdict was returned. He was hanged 7 months after Hickok's death.

- "Whether on foot or on horseback, he was one of the most perfect types of physical manhood I ever saw."
  – George A. Custer, speaking of Wild Bill Hickok

- "Pard, we will meet again in the happy hunting grounds to part no more." – written on the slab at the head of Wild Bill's grave

## Annie Oakley

- If the name Phoebe Ann Moses doesn't ring a bell as a Wild West legend, perhaps it is because she is better known by her stage name, Annie Oakley. Ohio-born Annie began sharpening her shooting skills out of necessity when she was required to supply meat for her poverty-stricken family after the deaths of her father, and later, stepfather. She soon became an expert shot, and at age 8, went to work for a Cincinnati hotel, killing game for its kitchen. She paid off her family's mortgage through this job and by selling animal pelts to a trapper.

- Annie Oakley met her future husband, Frank Butler, at age 15, when she competed against him in a shooting exhibition. Butler was considered the best marksman in the country, and this barely-five-foot-tall teen defeated him shooting live birds, netting $100 for her trouble. Butler was quite taken with her, and the following year they were married, and remained happily so for over 40 years.

- Annie Oakley became a headliner for Buffalo Bill's Wild West Show at age 25 She was always the image of the perfect lady. She did needlepoint in her spare time and often performed horseback tricks from a sidesaddle while wearing an ankle-length skirt. One of her tricks was to point her rifle backward over her shoulder while taking aim in a mirror, hitting targets placed behind her. She shot dimes out of her husband's hand and cigarettes out of his mouth, and apples off the head of her poodle, George. Out of 1,000 glass balls thrown into the air, she shattered 943. During her 1899 season, it is estimated that she fired 48,000 shots.

- It was Sitting Bull, now captured and part of Buffalo Bill's show, who dubbed Annie Oakley "Little Sure Shot."
- When Annie was 41, she was seriously injured in a head-on train collision, and, within 17 hours, her hair turned completely white. Told she would never move or shoot again, she endured five agonizing operations. After two years of willing herself to recover, she walked with a leg brace and a cane, and once again was able to shoot. She went on to tour with a theatrical group. She also instructed WWI soldiers in shooting techniques.
- When Annie died in 1926, her husband Frank refused to eat or sleep, and met her in eternity just 20 days later.
- "I think that sport and healthful exercise make women better, healthier, and happier" – Annie Oakley

## The James Brothers

- Beginning in Feb., 1866, Frank & Jesse James pulled off 26 robberies in 15 years, for about $500,000. Their first robbery brought them $60,000 and their first victim, a 19-year-old college student. Their take from subsequent holdups never reached the booty from their first.
- These two sons of a Baptist preacher served in the Confederate Army, where they learned many of their attack tactics. Frank was a fan of Shakespeare's writings.
- The James Brothers' career started with banks and added trains as time went by.
- After a close call during a bank robbery in Minnesota, from which only Frank and Jesse escaped, they hid out and settled

down with wives and families in Tennessee. Detectives were still on the lookout, and one actually unknowingly enjoyed a friendly chat with Jesse on a city street. Jesse later sent him a postcard informing him he had seen Jesse James in the flesh.

- After 5 years of refuge, the James Brothers started up a new gang and began a new killing and robbery rampage. It was one of their own gang members who had made a bargain with authorities and finally killed Jesse, shooting him in the head. The man pleaded guilty, was sentenced to death, and was then pardoned by the governor as part of his secret bargain. Fearing for his life, Frank James turned himself in and the only charge against him was one murder, after years of killing innocent citizens. Unbelievably he was acquitted, and lived to age 72.

- Legend has it that there are still hundreds of thousands of dollars in unrecovered gold from robberies committed by Frank and Jesse James buried somewhere in southwestern Oklahoma.

- "It's awfully hot today." – Jesse James' last words, directed at the friend who had just shot him

## Calamity Jane

- Martha "Calamity Jane" Canary moved to Deadwood, South Dakota, at age 23, in the midst of the area's gold rush. While romantic legend depicts her as a beautiful frontierswoman in buckskins, in truth, she was masculine-looking, dressed in men's clothing, and was a coarse, foul-mouthed, unwashed, cigar-smoking, tobacco-chewing, lawless alcoholic with yellow teeth, who often resorted to prostitution as a means of making a living. According to an acquaintance, she could "outswear any man in the place."

- Whatever else Calamity Jane was, she was an expert marksman. She loved the romantic biographies written about her, and more than likely, invented many of the stories herself. She often insisted that she was married to Wild Bill Hickok, although the only evidence is a written entry in a Bible, dated

1870. She claimed a daughter by Wild Bill, whom she named Jean, and gave up for adoption when Jean was 4. Supposedly, she gave Bill a divorce in Deadwood so he could marry Agnes Thatcher.

- One of the more complimentary truths about Calamity Jane were her heroic efforts at nursing victims of a smallpox epidemic in Deadwood in 1878, when townsfolk dubbed her "Heroine of the Hills." She was in fact lowered into her grave by a man she had nursed through the plague when he was a boy. One story goes that it was because of this time in her life that she earned the name "Calamity Jane," because she was always to be counted on when there was a calamity. However, there are many differing stories as to how she achieved her famous nickname.

- Calamity Jane's later years were a steady decline, including being fired from Buffalo Bill's Show for excessive drinking. When pneumonia finally took her life at age 51, she was penniless. Her last words were, "It's the 27th anniversary of Bill's death. Bury me next to Bill." She was placed in a new pine coffin, wearing a crisp white dress, and her last wish was indeed honored, as she and Wild Bill Hickok lie side by side in Mt. Moriah Cemetery in Deadwood.

## The Lone Ranger

- The Lone Ranger was actually Texas Ranger Reid, who earned his name by being the sole survivor of a bloody fight between a group of six Rangers and the "Hole-in-the-Wall" Butch Cavendish Gang. The Lone Ranger's brother, Captain Daniel Reid, was killed in the skirmish. The Lone Ranger, badly injured and left to die, was discovered by Tonto, who nurtured him back to health and dubbed him "The Lone Ranger."

- The Lone Ranger's disguise was the result of attempting to avoid recognition by the Cavendish Gang. The Lone Ranger's trademark silver bullets were the product of a silver mine owned by the Reid Brothers.

- Tonto named the Lone Ranger's white stallion Silver, because "his flanks shone like silver in the dazzling sun." The horse's shoes were also silver, another product of the Reid Brothers' silver mine.
- Tonto's Indian name for the Lone Ranger was "Kemo Sabay," which means "Faithful Friend."
- The Lone Ranger was an expert at disguises — prospector, cowboy, handsome foreigner — whatever was necessary to overcome his evil adversaries. Tall, well-built, deep-voiced, with chiseled features, and distinctive blue eyes, he was the epitome of the Old West lawman. Unfortunately, he never existed.

## Buffalo Bill Cody

- William Frederick Cody had many occupations before becoming the famous founder of the Wild West Show, including Pony Express rider at age 14, driver of horse teams during the Civil War, a hotel operator, freight business owner (which terminated when Indians stole his wagons and horses), land speculator, railroad construction worker, buffalo hunter, scout, and cattleman.
- It was while employed as a buffalo hunter, supplying meat for the workers building the Transcontinental Railroad, that Cody earned the nickname "Buffalo Bill." The year was 1867 and he killed 4,280 buffalo.
- Cody was 37 when he formed "Buffalo Bill's Wild West Show," which toured the U.S. and Europe, and included mock battles between Cavalry and Indians, as well as shooting and horsemanship demonstrations.
- Buffalo Bill received the Congressional Medal of Honor for his part in a skirmish with Indians along the Platte River. The Medal was later revoked by Congress because Cody was not in the military at the time.
- Although Buffalo Bill continued performing until two months before his death, he also operated a ranch in northwestern Wyoming.

- Hours before his death from uremic poisoning, Buffalo Bill requested to be baptized a Catholic and became one for less than a day.

## Last Bit

- The Gunfight at the O.K. Corral didn't even take place at the O.K. Corral, but in a nearby vacant lot. The gunfight was between the Earp brothers, Wyatt, Morgan, and Virgil, along with their 28-year-old quarrelsome, tubercular, alcoholic, gambling dentist friend, Doc Holliday, and the Clanton and McLaury Gangs. The gunfight lasted only 30 seconds. Although considered one of the "good guys," 31-year-old Wyatt had actually been a horse thief and a gambler before serving as Assistant Marshal to his older brother Virgil. In 1923, at age 75, Wyatt Earp was an adviser on the silent film, Wild Bill Hickok.

# INVENTIONS AND THEIR INVENTORS
by Mona McKown

- Definition: act of producing something new; an original contrivance.
- An invention often begins with one person's idea, but it usually does not stop with one person. Other people can make improvements on the invention to make it more useful.

## Accidental Inventions

- In 1839, Charles Goodyear accidentally dropped some natural rubber, which was mixed with sulfur, onto a hot stove. This accident created vulcanized rubber. It was tough and very elastic and it did not become brittle in cold weather or sticky in hot weather. Goodyear's chance invention would later prove to have hundreds of uses: from rainwear to automobile tires.

## Inventions Made At Home

- At age 10 Becky Schroeder, of Toledo, Ohio, invented the Glo-board in her home. She came up with the idea while waiting in the car for her mother. It was dark and she thought that it was too bad she did not have paper that would light up, so she could be doing her homework. Later, after thinking about her problem, she coated a piece of cardboard with glow-in-the-dark paint and then drew lines on it. To use the board she would lay a piece of paper over it and the glow would shine through the paper, enabling Becky to write in the dark.
- At age 13, Jonathan Santos of Bowie, Maryland, designed and made a cross-shaped boomerang. It returns to the thrower, hovers, and then floats gently down.

- Chester Greenwood, at age 15, invented Chester's Champion Ear Protectors out of personal necessity. He lived in Farmington, Maine, where the winters are quite cold. Chester loved to ice skate, but his ears were bothered by the below-freezing temperatures. While skating one day his ears began to hurt, and he decided he had to do something about this problem. He ran home and twisted some wire into two loops and had his grandmother sew some cloth over the wire. He then went back to his skating and placed his muffs over his ears. They worked and his ears stayed warm. Later Chester added a spring that would fit over his head to hold the muffs in place. In 1877, Chester Greenwood received a patent for his invention. He opened a factory to manufacture his earmuffs and sold millions.

## Inventions For Entertainment

- During the 1800's billiards was a popular table game. The balls for the game were carved from ivory and were very expensive. In 1863, a maker of billiard balls offered $10,000 to anyone who could create a substitute for the ivory balls. A printer from Albany, New York, named John Wesley Hyatt decided to try to win the $10,000. For several years he tried molding balls of sawdust and glue but was unsuccessful. Next he tried coating the balls with a liquid which would dry hard and smooth. The liquid was made by adding alcohol and ether to cotton treated with acids. This treated cotton was called nitrocellulose and was made by some other chemists. Hyatt did a lot of experimenting with the nitrocellulose but was unable to come up with the right combination. Finally inspiration hit! He mixed the treated cotton with camphor and alcohol, which left a moldable solid instead of a liquid. Hyatt then put the soft solid into a mold which he heated and put pressure to. After the mold cooled, Hyatt opened it and out popped the first molded plastic. Finally after seven years Hyatt accomplished what he had set out to do. Unfortunately, though, the $10,000 offer had expired. Hyatt's celluloid, as he called it, did open up a whole new industry with many uses.

- Cartoons have been around for centuries, but the modern-day cartoon is a long way from its ancestors. Originally the word "cartoon" was used by painters during the Italian Renaissance. It referred to the first sketch in actual size of any work of art which covered a large area. Later when magazines and newspapers began to use drawings to illustrate news and to provide amusement, these drawings were also called "cartoons." The first comic strips appeared in the early 1900's. Buster Brown was created by Richard Outcault and appeared as a comic strip in 1902.

- The first jigsaw puzzle was invented by an Englishman around 1760. John Spilsbury was trying to come up with a way for children to learn their geography more easily. Spilsbury painted slabs of wood with various regional maps and then cut the wood along the boundary lines. This idea then led others to the puzzles that are popular today.

## Inventions We Take For Granted

- Charles F. Kettering was tired of trying to start his automobile with the cumbersome and dangerous hand-crank. So in 1910, Kettering and his assistants worked day and night for almost a year to develop a small battery-powered motor which would start the engine of a car with the mere press of a button.

- Many inventors have been involved in the development of the "Band-Aid." In a Philadelphia medical journal of 1830,

Samuel D. Gross reported his use of medicated adhesive plasters for body fractures. In 1845, Dr. Thomas Allcock marketed Allock's Porous Plaster. It was an adhesive plaster painted with rubber dissolved in a solvent. Dr. Horace H. Day and Dr. William H. Shecut of New Jersey were the two men to patent this invention. In 1874, Robert W. Johnson and George J. Seabury developed a medicated adhesive plaster with a rubber base. In 1886, Johnson left Seabury to set up his own business, Johnson and Johnson, and his Band-Aids with their rubber base hit the jackpot commercially.

- In 1892, Joshua Pusey, of Lima, Pennsylvania, was the man responsible for the creation of book matches. He took out a patent on the idea and four years later he sold his patent to the Diamond Match Company of Barberton, Ohio. The book matches did not really catch on until 1896 when a brewery ordered 10 million of them to use for advertising.

- Toilet paper was created by Joseph C. Gayetty in 1857. Gayetty created an "unbleached pearl-colored pure manila hemp paper" and had his name "watermarked on each sheet." "Gayetty's Medicated Paper," as it was marketed and advertised claimed to be "a perfectly pure article for the toilet and for the prevention of piles." This first toilet paper came in 500-sheet packages and sold for 50 cents.

- While incarcerated in a cell of England's Newgate Prison, William Addis invented the first toothbrush. While in prison, Addis had little to do, but think. He was trying to think of a way to make a living once his sentence had been completed. One morning after washing his face, he began to clean his teeth with a rag. This was the acceptable method in 1770. Addis, however, considered this practice to be ineffective and by the next day had come up with a solution. He saved a small bone from some meat he had been served and drilled tiny holes in it. He then acquired some hard bristles, cut them down, tied them into tufts and glued the tufts into the holes. Eureka, the first toothbrush. When he was released from prison, Addis went into the toothbrush-manufacturing business. Instantaneously, he was successful.

- The first flexible straw was invented by Joseph B. Friedman of Santa Monica, California, in 1938, after watching the frustration his young daughter experienced when her soda straw kept bending over the rim of her glass. Friedman thought that a corrugated section in the straw would produce a better drinking implement. He called his straw the Flex-Straw. It could be used in either hot or cold liquids and was much cleaner than the earlier straws, which were made of paraffined manila paper.

- The Paper Clip was invented in the 1900's by a Norwegian named Johann Vaaler, who first bent a piece of wire into a double oblong shape and then solved the problem of how to hold loose papers together. However, it was later patented in Germany and is a rare example of an invention that has scarcely been improved. The only significant development was made in the 1950's in Britain when the design was changed by bending the tip of the inner oblong upward to make it easier to guide onto the papers it was to hold.

- In 1903, Albert J. Parkhouse worked for the Timberlake Wire and Novelty Company of Jackson, Michigan. The company manufactured lampshade frames and other wire items. Parkhouse noticed that when the men working at the factory went to hang their coats up, there were not a sufficient number of hooks available to hang them and the coats that were hung up would wrinkle. So Parkhouse picked up a piece of wire, bent it into two large oblong hoops opposite each other, and twisted both ends at the center, where a hook had been formed by twisting the middle together. He then bent the loops up slightly so the coat hanging on it would stay on. The company thought it was such a good idea they took out a patent on it. Parkhouse never received a penny for his wire coat hanger invention.

- In 1778, Joseph Bramah, a London cabinet-maker, began the first production of water closets (toilets). The bowl was completely hidden by surrounding wood. Between 1778 and 1797 he sold around 6,000 units.
- In 1948, a Swiss engineer, George de Mistral was on a hunting trip in the Alps. As he was walking, he noticed several burrs caught in his hunting dog's ears. After taking a closer look at the burr he discovered that there were tiny hooks on each one clinging to the hairs on his dog. This gave him the idea for a new fastener. Fifteen years later he introduced Velcro.

## Inventive Quotes

- "The art of invention grows young with things invented."
  – Francis Bacon
- "Human subtlety...will never devise an invention more beautiful, more simple or more direct than does nature, because in her inventions nothing is lacking, and nothing is superfluous." – Leonardo da Vinci
- "Necessity is the mother of invention."
  – Anonymous Latin saying
- "Very learned women are to be found, in the same manner as female warriors; but they are seldom or never inventors."
  – Voltaire
- "The greatest invention of the nineteenth century was the invention of the method of invention."
  – Alfred North Whitehead
- "Invention breeds invention. No sooner is the electric telegraph devised that gutta percha, the very material it requires, is found." – Ralph Waldo Emerson
- "The marvel of modern technology include the development of a soda can which, when discarded, will last forever – and a $7,000 car, which, when properly cared for, will rust out in two or three years." – Paul Harwitz
- "It is providential that the youth or man of inventive mind is not 'blessed' with a million dollars. The mind is sharper and keener in seclusion and uninterrupted solitude. Originality

thrives in seclusion free of outside influences beating upon us to cripple the creative mind. Be alone – that is the secret of invention: be alone, that is when ideas are born."                      – Nikola Tesla

- "I just invent, then wait until man comes around to needing what I've invented."          – R. Buckminster Fuller
- "We owe a lot to Thomas Edison – if it wasn't for him, we'd be watching television by candlelight."
                              – Milton Berle

## The Last Look

- Donald Duck and his three nephews, Huey, Dewey, and Louie are credited with inventing a way to raise a sunken ship. In the 1949 Walt Disney Comic book, they raised a sunken yacht by filling it full of Ping-Pong balls. In 1964, a Danish manufacturer, Karl Kroyer, ordered 27 billion polystyrene balls to be injected into the hull of the Al Kuwait, which was a freighter that had capsized in the harbor of Kuwait. The freighter had a cargo of 6,000 sheep, and local citizens feared that the rotting carcasses would poison their supply of drinking water. The freighter was successfully raised and Kuwait's water supply was saved. Few people realize that the great engineering feat was made possible by cartoonist Carl Barks and his fictional ducks.

# HISTORICAL HYSTERIA

by V.B. Darrington

### The First Fact

- The inventor of the toilet was an Englishman. His invention so impressed the queen that she knighted him. His name is proudly in the history books, Sir Thomas Crapper.

### It Happened Way Back When

- The highest temperature recorded on Earth was 136 degrees in the shade. The hot spot was in Libya in 1922.
- Joan of Arc was burned at the stake after having been convicted of being a witch. But, that wasn't the only crime with which she had been charged. She was also accused of disobeying her parents.
- Mark Twain lived in the shadow of cosmic destiny. He was born when Haley's comet was bright in the sky. He died 75 years later, when the comet made its next visit.
- Tycho Brahe, the famous Danish astronomy pioneer, may not have been born with a silver spoon in his mouth, but he eventually acquired a nose of gold. The dashing scientist lost the tip of his nose in a duel and had a prosthesis fashioned out of gold.
- Chocolate lovers watched in agony as the Blommer Chocolate Factory caught fire in 1980. Inside the blaze, 100-pound bags of chocolate melted and formed huge chocolate ponds and streams. The struggling firemen slipped and fell in the slick liquid, over and over again. When the fire was finally out, many of the firefighters resembled huge chocolate-dipped Easter treats.

- Animals have had their day in court. In old Italy it was not uncommon for a pig or a horse to be brought to the tribunal for killing its owner. The unfortunate animals usually faced the death penalty if found guilty.
- At least one U.S. court has held council on an animal defendant. In South Bend, Indiana, a chimpanzee made the mistake of smoking a cigarette in a public street. In 1902, that was not allowed. The chimp was arrested, tried in court, and found guilty. The chimpanzee belonged to a traveling carnival worker, who paid the fine and purchased the monkey's freedom.
- Pirates wore earrings because they believed the holes in their ears improved their vision.

G. WENZEL

- One hundred years ago, only one in six families owned a bathtub. In fact, it wasn't until after the first World War that tubs could be found in more than 50 per cent of American homes. Bathing was considered unhealthful by much of the general public. Even many medical professionals would prescribe baths only as a drastic therapy. In the Old West, a portable tub was designed out of canvas. The tub was shaped like a large bag, with a collar that fit around one's neck. The contraption was "worn" by the bather while sitting in a chair.

- Leno and Letterman have a long way to go. It is estimated that Johnny Carson cracked over 600,000 jokes while he was the host of <u>The Tonight Show</u>.

- In 1823, a citizen of Cincinnati checked out a book from the University's Medical Library. He neglected to return it. His great-grandson returned the book 145 years later. The librarian figured the overdue fine at $2,264. Kindly, he excused the great-grandson from paying the fee.

- John Smith was saved by the beautiful Pocahontas – or was he? Apocryphal history would have us believe that John Smith was captured by Native Americans and sentenced to die. At the crucial moment, the 12-year-old Pocahontas rushed forward, interceding on behalf of the White man. In actual fact, John Smith never mentioned Pocahontas in his initial writings about Jamestown. It wasn't until several years later that John Smith reported the legendary incident. Among his friends, Smith was known as an inventive storyteller. And on more than one occasion he claims to have been rescued by beautiful young women.

- The witch hunt of 1692 was a bad time to live in Salem. It started when several young girls listened to stories of witchcraft from the mouth of a slave named Tituba. For days afterwards, the girls had screaming fits and nightmares. In their fits, the girls shouted out the names of neighbors who lived in Salem. The townsfolk believed that the names were obviously those of witches. Trials were held for thirty people. Twenty people were found guilty, nineteen of whom were hanged, and one of whom was pressed to death under stones.

- A man named Thomas Adams discovered chewing gum while attempting to find a substitute for rubber. Adams had surmised that chicle, the sap of the sapodilla tree, might fill the bill. He happened to chew a bit of the sap and found it to his liking.

Adams added sweeteners and flavors to the chicle gum and marketed it in the U.S. At first, the idea was an abject flop. People didn't understand the point of chewing something without swallowing it. Eventually, Adams authorized candy shops to offer the chicle free with purchases of other candy items. By 1890, Thomas Adams was a wealthy man.

## Miscellany Mania

- Next time you contemplate the "Mona Lisa", look carefully: perhaps her smile isn't the only thing that gives her that enigmatic charm. You see, Mona doesn't have any eyebrows. Like all the fine noblewomen of her time, she shaved her eyebrows for vanity.

- Buckingham Palace is where the Queen of England calls home. The palace boasts 602 rooms.

- Drop a raisin in a glass of soda or champagne. The raisin will sink and then slowly begin to rise. When it reaches the top, it will sink again, and the process will repeat itself.

- If you've ever suffered in high heels, imagine what Cinderella must have felt like in glass slippers. In fact, Cinderella's slippers were actually made of fur. Our present misconception occurred many years ago when the story was translated from French to English.

- In Iceland, many inhabitants share the same last name. As a result, names are listed in the phone directory first names before last.

- A frog cannot swallow without closing its eyes. Apparently, this is the frog's built-in defense mechanism against having its eyes damaged by struggling prey. Many four-year-olds practice the same defense when slurping spaghetti.

- The world's largest tree is the General Sherman Sequoia in California. The tree stands as tall as a 20-story building and weighs more than 2,000 tons.

- Phobias are irrational fears, but they don't seem that way to the sufferer. Some of the most exotic phobias are as follows: chromophobia-fear of colors; sitophobia-fear of food;

arachibutyrophobia-fear of peanut butter sticking to the roof of one's mouth.

- A typewriter in America has 43 keys and 84 symbols. In China, a typewriter has only one key. The single key is moved over a large platen to activate 2,500 symbols.

- Chanan Singh is famous for his unique skill. The Indian artist paints pictures on grains of rice. His steady hands guide minute paintbrushes in creating beautiful landscapes and portraits that can be appreciated only with a magnifying glass. Chanan admits that he is always afraid that one of his masterpieces might be accidentally eaten.

- Next Valentine's Day, send your valentine card to the postmaster in "Loveland," Colorado. The post office there will re-send your love letter to your sweetheart, after stamping it with a special cancel stamp bearing a romantic poem and a small red cowboy. But remember to mail early. The Loveland post office handles nearly 250,000 valentines each year.

- Most of the vanilla that we eat is actually an artificial substitute. The genuine article is extracted from long, slender bean pods. Real vanilla is quite expensive. In Madagascar, the crop is so valuable that the bean growers actually brand each pod. Growers are assigned numbers which they carefully burn into each pod to discourage "bean rustlers."

- Pigs are often maligned as dirty, smelly animals. In fact, a breed of pot-bellied pigs is making a popular house pet. The owners say the animals are clean and very affectionate. Experts assert that pigs are as intelligent as dogs.

- Our sense of smell is pathetic compared to that of the rest of the animal kingdom. A bloodhound, for example, is capable of distinguishing the different scent of different people, even after several days or after rain. However, in some human cultures, where the sense of smell is valuable for hunting, the natives develop surprising olfactory abilities. U.S. servicemen, on a survival training exercise in the South Pacific, were puzzled at how quickly the natives were able to track them out of hiding. The Islanders laughingly gave away the secret of their hide-and-seek success. The U.S. airmen smelled of soap.

- In other countries, the lunch hour lasts as much as two hours. It is even common for factories, stores, and traffic to come to a standstill. Americans don't seem to have the same respect for digestion; a half-hour lunch is almost a national standard. In the U.S. we also frequently eat on the street, as we drive, or while doing business. In some other cultures, it is considered taboo to eat in public.

- In 1986, a veterinarian in Florida was surprised when a lumpy snake was brought to his surgery. The snake had swallowed two 15-watt light bulbs from a trash bin; apparently it had mistaken them for eggs. The bulbs were extracted and the snake recovered.

- Most Americans come factory-equipped with brown hair, nearly 70 percent. Only about 15 percent are naturally blond. A still smaller segment of the population, 10 percent, has black hair. The rarest people are the 5 percent with red hair.

- Recently, a radio talk show host was angered by the fact that someone had attempted to register a pig as a presidential candidate. The host railed that a pig was incapable of doing the job. "They just sit around all day," he said. "Anyone knows they should have registered it for vice-president!"

- Rice is the primary staple-food of more than half the world's inhabitants.

- An average American who lives to the age of 70 will have eaten a lot of meat: 880 chickens, 14 beef cattle, 23 pigs, 35 turkeys, 12 sheep, and 770 pounds of fish.

- Catsup, or ketchup, came to us from China by way of Great Britain. The Chinese made a spicy fish sauce that was adopted by the Britons. The British added tomatoes to the mix, and our present day sauce was born. Catsup was sold as medicine back in the early 1830's.

- Astronauts on the space shuttle bathe in a strange manner.

They shower in a sealed cabinet similar to a small car wash. The astronauts are first sprayed with water, and then they are air-dried by jets of compressed gas. These extraordinary measures are required because of the dangerous potential that water has for damaging the spacecraft. Even the tiniest drops of escaped water would form into spheres and drift weightlessly throughout the cabin, possibly fouling electrical equipment.

## The Final Fact

- One million dollars in $100 bills weighs just around twenty pounds. One billion dollars weighs 10 tons.

# ECCENTRICS
by J. C. Walker

- **ec'cen'tric** (ik'sen'trik) – "departing from the center; of a whimsical temperament; one who defies the social conventions; departure from normal way of conducting oneself; not placed, or not having the axis placed, centrally."

*The New Webster's Dictionary*

## Excedrin Headache #248

- Eccentrics come in all shapes, sizes, colors, and perforations. One interesting group out there believes ardently in a procedure known as trepanning. The theory is that drilling a substantial-sized hole in the top of one's head improves mental function, relieves stress, and releases the potential for development of all facets of the personality. The Society for Trepanning is for real and publishes a magazine, not for review by the squeamish, called <u>The Auger</u>. To substantiate their claims, the group presents a thorough bibliography from archeological journals showing that trephination has been performed on humans for thousands of years and in a variety of cultures.

- Trepanning can also be a do-it-yourself project. A woman in London recently reported having drilled a hole in her skull to test the theory that increased blood flow to the top of the head would cause her brain to function more efficiently. She admitted to using a local anesthetic, and stated, "I feel calmer, and that particular mental exhaustion I became so used to has gone."

## Wedge-Free

- An uncomfortable engineer recently patented a design for jockey shorts he claims is vastly superior. He calls them E2U – Ergonomically Engineered Underwear.

- "Great spirits have always found violent opposition from mediocre minds. The latter cannot understand it when a man does not thoughtlessly submit to hereditary prejudices but honestly and courageously uses his intelligence."

– Albert Einstein

## Just Do It Anyway

- Scottish eccentric John Slater definitely marches to the beat of a different drummer. He resides in a cave in the highlands, but often takes to the highway, which is where he gets most of the media attention he receives. He recently walked 750 miles, from England to Scotland, wearing pajamas and no shoes.

## No Discouraging Word

- Then again, some of us are meant to share our unique vision of the world with others. In 1993, the image of a giant buffalo emerged on the plains of northeast Wyoming. Sculptor Robert Berks directed the movement of a tractor with a walkie-talkie as the vehicle methodically dropped bales of straw as he specified targets. Berks then marked the straw with red dye – within four days a picture one half mile long and a third of a mile wide became recognizable as that of an American bison. The artist has no plans to stop there, however; his next part of the plan is to make the drawing permanent with stone outlines fifty feet across.Then he anticipates filling in the outline with one thousand weather vanes the size and shape of buffalo. He chose this number because that was the usual size of a herd in the days before their near-extermination. The expression "buffalo herd" will take on new meaning, too – he expects eventually to outfit each weather vane with special tubing that will bellow as the wind blows through it, presumably a sound reminiscent of the buffalo themselves.

- The eccentric made an appointment with the psychiatrist, and appeared at the reception desk wearing a purple football jersey, a seventeenth century cape and a Napoleon hat. On his feet were cowboy boots with spurs that jingled when he walked, and tied around his waist was a braided silk rope which dragged a toy fire engine behind him. In one hand

he held a lollipop and in the other a candied apple. "I need to see the Doctor right away," he said to the startled receptionist. "I must speak to him about my brother."

## Bull Market

- Many highly successful corporation executives are often considered to be eccentric. If qualities such as intellectual curiosity, independent work habits, and often unjustified optimism are considered essential, then that may account for these individuals' success in the first place. The second richest man in the United States, financier Warren Buffett, is regarded as eccentric because he likes to wear cheap suits, eat hamburgers, drink cherry Coke, and live in Omaha. Rodney East, former head of a company called Etam, didn't work out of an office but rather carried his files around in a brown paper bag. A newspaper heir named Gordon Bennett, when dining out, used to love to pull the tablecloths out from under the dishes at neighboring tables, then generously pay for the damages.

- There was loud and frantic knocking on the door and the eccentric doctor answered it. "Doc, please, you have to come right away," said the man. "It's my son – he breaks thermometers, drinks the mercury, and throws the glass on the floor!" "What!?" yelled the doctor. "That's the best part!"

## Progress Marches On

- While many Nobel prize winners may be a little preoccupied with their work, most are with-it enough to contribute scientific findings that ultimately help humankind. It's reassuring to know that scientists who contribute absolutely nothing of signficant social importance are now recognized, too. Harvard University annually presents its Ig Nobel prizes for "achievements that cannot or should not be reproduced." Recent winners were noted for their work in proving toast always falls butter-side down, the effect of ale, garlic and sour cream on the appetite of leeches, and how to light a barbeque in under 5 seconds using only charcoal and liquid oxygen. Non-scientists are honored, too. This year the academy commemorated the inventor of the pink lawn flamingo with the Ig Nobel in Art, as well as the tobacco industry with the Ig Nobel for Medicine for "their unshakable discovery...that nicotine is not addictive."

## Don't Leave Home Without It

- Walter Cavenaugh carries 1,394 credit cards in his wallet, which weighs 38 pounds. He estimates the cards are good for $1.65 million in credit.

- The eccentric novelist had a bad case of writer's block for several years, so his publicist was thrilled when he learned he'd begun work on a new book. For three months the agent would call to check on the novelist's progress, and he always assured him great strides were being made. One day the writer phoned the publicist and informed him the book was finished and that he would send him the manuscript the following week. When the package arrived at his office, he eagerly tore open the package and began to read. "General Jones leaped up on his faithful horse and yelled, 'Giddyup, giddyup, giddyup, giddyup.'" The publicist leafed through the rest of the document and picked up the phone. "There's nothing here but five hundred pages of 'giddyups!'" he screamed at the writer. "Yeah," said the man. "Stubborn horse."

## Mouth Off

- And then there are the fifteen minutes of eccentric fame that we ordinary folks can claim. Among the most notable are these:
- Susan Montgomery Williams, who blew the world's largest bubble-gum bubble in supervised competition in Fresno, California, in 1994. It had a diameter of 23 inches.
- Al Gliniecki of Pensacola, Florida, captured the world's championship for tying cherry stems into knots with his tongue – 833 of them – in one hour.
- The record for catching a grape thrown into the air and caught by mouth is held by Paul J. Tavilla in East Boston, Massachusetts, in 1991. His friend threw the grape 327 1/2 feet up, although there is no report as to how he substantiated the distance.

## Marriage Made In Heaven

- A bride in Missouri recently decided she wanted a wedding that was really different. Rather than taking a limousine to her ceremony, Terri Essex jumped from an airplane 10,000 feet above the heads of her guests and her husband-to-be. Her father, who was pleased she decided to combine her wedding with his annual fly-in barbeque, officially gave his daughter away by encouraging her to jump from the airplane door. After landing in her first jump ever, Terri peeled off the flight suit to reveal her wedding dress. The event proceeded without further delay.

## That First Step's A Doozy

- A man recently sued Disneyland because he fell from the skyway gondola ride. Fortunately, he landed in a tree and received only minor injuries. Later he thought better of his lawsuit in which he claimed he had "come out" of the gondola, even though the park officials said that could not easily have happened since the door latch was on the outside of the door and was thoroughly tested to determine if it could have opened accidently. He admitted his suit was "ill-advised." The park removed the ride, which had been in operation since the park opened in 1956.

## There Goes The Neighborhood

- A real estate agent in Chico, California, has the listing of a lifetime – three sixties-era missile silos on 51.2 acres of pasture, perfect for renovation as a vacation getaway. It's priced for a quick sale at $1.8 million, and the agent's sales pitch is that it could be a recording studio for a rock artist, a sacred underground shrine, or simply a piece of treasured Cold War nostalgia.

## To Coin A Phrase

- If you're casting about for a new hobby to add meaning to your life, consider taking up coin snatching. The world's record for coin snatching is held by an Englishman named Dean Gould, who caught 328 out of 482 British 10-pence coins (about the size of a quarter) in 1993. His highly-skilled technique includes a careful stacking technique which links columns of coins together so they will hold together as they're caught. The real trick is that the snatcher stacks the coins on his or her bent forearm, which rests parallel to the chin. The arm is dropped and as many of the interconnected coins as possible are caught in mid-air. Preparation takes about 20 minutes while the coins are slowly stacked in columns on the arm.

## Live Long And Prosper

- Believe it or not, planets can be eccentric, too. That's what they're called when they have an irregular orbit or do just plain unexplainable things. A mysterious "planet" appeared in astronomers' telescopes in 1859 (a very big year for eccentrics) as they gazed at the surface of the sun, and there was instant speculation that an undiscovered moon of Mercury had been revealed. The body mysteriously disappeared, however, and modern scientists believe it was probably an asteroid, which astronomers didn't know existed then. The "eccentric planet" earned its own place in history, though, when the excited 19th century star-gazers named it Vulcan.

- The eccentric walked into the diner and ordered a cup of coffee. He then proceeded to put twenty heaping spoonfuls of sugar into the cup, carefully picked it up and began to sip very small sips.

  "Why don't you stir it?" said the confused waitress.

  "Why should I?" the man replied. "I don't like it sweet."

# THE MONTH OF DECEMBER
by Kathy Wolfe

## First Fact

- If the Latin word <u>Decem</u> means "ten," and a decade is ten years, and the decathlon is ten different track and field events, and a decagon has ten sides, why is December the twelfth month rather than the tenth? Actually, it is the tenth month, although not in our present Gregorian calendar. It was the tenth month in the Roman calendar, and originally had only 29 days. It was Julius Caesar who gave it the two additional days.

## Bits About The Month

- It was also an early Roman calendar which first listed Dec. 25 as the birthday of Jesus Christ, and coincided with pagan celebrations held to observe the end of harvest. Christmas was actually outlawed in England, as it was considered a pagan festival because of its many non-Christian customs.
- December contains the shortest day of the year, December 21, the first day of Winter, when the sun has reached its most southerly position. This is called the Winter Solstice. While we in the Northern Hemisphere experience the shortest day of the year, those in the Southern Hemisphere have their longest day. For this reason, many Australians spend their Christmas holiday on a picnic at the beach.

## These Things Happened

- In Dec., 1982, Heisman Trophy winner and pro-football player Herschel Walker was out for his morning jog. He stopped only to save the life of a 67-year-old woman caught in a burning automobile before continuing his workout.

- It was 25-year-old Mark David Chapman who gunned down former Beatle John Lennon in front of Lennon's residence in New York City on Dec. 8, 1980. Lennon had recently released his first album in five years.

- On Dec. 17,1903, Kitty Hawk, North Carolina, was the site of the world's first successful airplane flight . While Orville Wright made the first flight of 120 feet, his brother Wilbur made the longest flight that same day at 852 feet. The plane's speed was about 30 mph. Since the flights were witnessed by only five people (four men and a boy), the event went largely unnoticed and the story failed to attract the interest of the local newspaper. It was five years before the brothers' accomplishments became widely known. Today's 747 jumbo jet's wingspan is longer than Orville's first flight.

- The world's first human heart transplant was performed in December, 1967, by a South African surgeon, Christiaan Barnard. A 55-year-old man received the heart of a 25-year-old woman killed in an auto accident. The patient, Louis Washkansky, lived for 18 days before succumbing to a lung infection.

- About 3,700 people were killed on Dec. 7, 1941, when Japan attacked Pearl Harbor that peaceful Sunday morning. The U.S. Pacific Fleet had 8 battleships anchored at Pearl Harbor, four of which were soon at the bottom of the sea. Nearly 200 planes were destroyed. President Franklin D. Roosevelt, along with the countries of Canada and Great Britain, declared war on Japan the next day. FDR stated that Dec. 7 was a "date which will live in infamy." Infamy, by the way, means "extreme wickedness."

- The U.S.S. Arizona, sunk in Pearl Harbor, remains the final resting place for more than 1,000 men.

- The birthstone for December is the turquoise, found in large amounts in Nevada and New Mexico. It is formed primarily by the wearing down of lava and receives its bluish color from its richness in copper.

## Holiday Facts

- During the twelve days of Christmas, your true love plans to bestow many gifts on you, according to the well-known song. If you receive them all, 23 birds will be your new pets — seven swans, six geese, four calling birds, three French hens, two turtledoves, and a partridge.

- Hanukkah is the Jewish Festival of Lights, a feast lasting eight days. The eight branches of the candleholder, called a menorah, contain candles that are lit, one per night of the feast. The taller middle candle of the menorah is called the shamash and is used to light the other eight.

- The miracle remembered at Hanukkah is that a small container of oil, needed to light the lamp to rededicate the Temple, was found, but was enough for only one day. However, miraculously it burned for eight days, hence the name "Festival of Lights." This feast followed a victorious battle by Jewish men for religious freedom.

- Eaten at Hanukkah, Latkes are pancakes made from grated potatoes.

- In Dec., 1975, Werner Erhard of San Francisco mailed out 62,824 Christmas cards, to give him the record for the most cards sent out by an individual.

- In 1977, then-President Jimmy Carter mailed out 60,000 cards. When Eisenhower was President in 1956, he could think of only 1,300 individuals to whom he needed to send Christmas greetings.

- If you want your holiday greetings to have a festive postmark, travel to Santa Claus, Indiana, population 927, to mail them. You'll be adding to the over 500,000 other pieces of mail that already pour into this town in the southern part of the state during the month of December. Legend has it that the town was named by settlers on Christmas Eve of 1852.

- A popular beverage during the holiday season is wassail, which consists of fruit juice or wine mixed with spices. The word originates from a Saxon phrase <u>was haile</u>, which means "Be healthy."
- The song "Rudolph the Red-Nosed Reindeer" was first sung in 1949 by Gene Autry at Madison Square Garden. It has since been recorded by over 500 different performers. Autry was also the first to record "Frosty the Snow Man."
- Before you sit down to gorge yourself on holiday dinners, remember that according to recent studies, only 4% of Americans are happy with their physical appearance.
- And as you're enjoying your roast turkey, consider that at the first Christmas feasts, people roasted boars, pigs, or peacocks.
- The popular holiday plant, the poinsettia, is a native of Mexico, and does especially well in tropical regions. As a potted plant it reaches a height of only around 3 feet, but outdoors it can grow to 15 feet tall. Although not fatal if eaten, the leaves can cause severe abdominal cramps. The plant's sap causes irritation if skin is exposed to it.
- Holly is actually an evergreen tree, with shiny leaves and bright red berries. The berries, which are poisonous, are classified as "drupes," which is fruit with a pit, as are peaches, plums, and cherries. The very hard wood of the holly tree is used in making musical instruments and furniture.
- Old English superstition was that holly had special powers to guard against witchcraft. Fastening it on the bedpost at Christmas protected people from the Evil One.
- The Boeing Air-craft Company's 1979 Christmas party is the largest on record, attended by 103,152 people in two shifts at Seattle's Kingdome.
- "Jingle Bells" was written 139 years ago.
- Although many Christians refuse to use the term "Xmas" to refer to Christmas, feeling it degrades the name of Christ, "X" is actually the first letter of Christ's name in the Greek

language, from which the abbreviation comes.
- It is Tiny Tim, a young crippled boy, who has the last word in Dickens' A Christmas Carol — the last five words, to be exact: "God Bless Us, Every One!"

## Around The World

- The Netherlands and Belgium celebrate St. Nicholas Day on Dec. 6. If you leave your shoes by the fireplace on the evening of Dec. 5, St. Nicholas will leave gifts in them. The negative side of this legend is that St. Nicholas often brings along Black Pete, who is in charge of whipping naughty children with his birch rod.

- Dec. 13 marks the beginning of the Christmas season in Sweden. This is St. Lucia Day, when the oldest girl in the family dresses all in white, wears a wreath of seven candles on her head, and brings the family breakfast in bed.
- A certain Russian gentleman by the name of Rudolph sat gazing out his window one dreary morning and remarked to his wife, "It's raining," to which she replied, "No, it's sleeting." However, her husband insisted, "Rudolph the Red knows rain, dear."
- If you're in Italy on Dec. 25, you are likely to hear wishes of Buon Natale. In Denmark, "Merry Christmas" is Glaedelig Jul, in Greece it's Kala Christougenna, and in Germany, Fr'hliche Weinachten.
- If the organ hadn't broken down at St. Nicholas Church in Oberndorf, Austria, in 1818, we might not have the beloved Christmas carol, "Silent Night." Father Joseph Mohr asked

the organist, Franz Gruber, to compose music for the words Father Mohr had written that could be sung to guitar music. It was not until 13 years later that it became well-known.

- Folks began decorating Christmas trees in their homes around the 1830's. In earlier years, the Christmas tree was not put up until Christmas Eve after the children had gone to bed, creating the belief that Santa had brought the presents AND the tree.

- Merchants' commercialization of Christmas caused one young lad to conclude, "By the time Christmas comes, I'm sick and tired of it."

- If you're asked to sing "Adeste Fidelis" during the holiday season and you're not familiar with the Latin lyrics, you can opt for the English of "O Come All Ye Faithful."

- The day after Christmas in England is called "Boxing Day," but is not related to that sport. It began in the Middle Ages when priests would empty the offering boxes in the church on Dec. 26 and give the contents to the poor. It continues to be the tradition today.

## The Man In The Red Suit

- The legend of Santa Claus developed from a real man, St. Nicholas, born in Turkey, who, at 19, became a priest, and later in life, a bishop. The legend goes that St. Nick helped a poor man with three daughters who had no dowries for any of them. St. Nick supposedly threw three bags of money into the man's house through the window, enabling the girls to marry. St. Nick then became the one who brings gifts on a special day, and in later years, on Christmas.

- The poem entitled "An Account of a Visit from St. Nicholas" is better known by its first line "'Twas the Night Before Christmas," and is credited to Clement Clarke Moore, a Biblical scholar and seminary professor, who supposedly wrote the poem as an 1822 Christmas gift to his children, although it did not appear in print until the following Christmas. Before this poem was published, St. Nicholas was pictured as a tall, dignified man in a bishop's robe, riding a white horse. It was cartoonist Thomas Nast who first illustrated St. Nick as the jolly fat man in the fur-trimmed suit, driving a sleigh pulled by reindeer. The name "Santa Claus" does not appear in Moore's poem.

# BASEBALL
by Mona McKown

## How Things Have Changed!

- Before 1859, the umpire at a baseball game would sit in a padded rocking chair behind the catcher.
- In the 1886 World Series there were a total of 63 errors made.
- Between the years of 1840 and 1850 a fielder would put out a runner by hitting him with the ball. There was also no distinction between fair and foul balls.
- The bases on a baseball field were arranged in a U-shape before 1845. The bases were made of posts or stakes. Runs were called "aces," and the team to reach a score of 21 was declared the winner. The game of baseball was more of a social event than a competitive sport even in the 1860's. Tea was served during intermissions, and the pitcher would throw the ball wherever the batter asked.

## Baseball Firsts

- Federic Rahr developed the first yellow baseball, first used on April 27, 1938, in New York City at the Columbia-Fordham game.
- The first major league All-star baseball game was played July 6, 1933, at Comiskey Park in Chicago. The National League was defeated by the American League with a score of 4-2. The attendance to the game was 49,200 fans, with gate receipts totaling $56,378.50.
- Contrary to popular belief, Abner Doubleday did not invent baseball. Articles about the game were issued as early as 1835. Doubleday, however, was only sixteen years of age at that

time. He is credited with inventing baseball in Cooperstown, New York, in 1839, but it is also a fact that he was enrolled in West Point from 1838 to 1842. At that time, a cadet from West Point was not allowed to leave the campus until the last years of his schooling. Therefore, he could not have been to Cooperstown before 1841.

- Charles G. Waite was a first baseman for a Boston team and in the late 1800's introduced the first baseball glove. This glove was unpadded.

- On March 15, 1869, the Cincinnati Red Stockings became the first professional baseball team.

- Pete Adelis was probably baseball's first "professional" heckler. He was six feet tall, weighed 260 pounds and wore a size fifty-two suit. He was nicknamed "Leather Lung Pete" or "the Iron Lung." He started his heckling career as a fan of the Philadelphia Athletics. He was very "scientific" in his heckling. He would study each player carefully and learn about the areas that were most sensitive to him. He did so well at his job that the management decided to start picking up his expenses so he could travel to the away-games and help distract the opposing team. This position continued until the 1950's when the Yankees hired Adelis away from the National League.

## Little League

- In Williamsport, Pennsylvania, the first Little League Baseball Program was formed. There were three teams. Today, however, the program is worldwide, involving 2-1/2 to 3 million girls and boys ranging in age from 8 to 18. The program involves slightly more than 9,000 leagues.

## Major League Records

- Pete Rose has the record for the most games played. He has played 3, 562 games with a record 14,053 at-bats.

- The record for the fastest base runner is held by Ernest Swanson, who in 1932 averaged a speed of 18.45 mph while circling the bases in 13.3 seconds.

- Stephen Koschal of Boynton Beach, Florida, owns the largest wooden baseball bat in the United States. It measures 5 feet 8-1/4 inches high and 22-3/4 inches wide and weighs 57-1/2 pounds. It also has the autographs of all the living members of the Baseball Hall of Fame on it.
- The youngest major league player was Joe Nuxhall, who was a pitcher for the Cincinnati Reds. He played one game in June 1944 at the age of 15 years 314 days.
- The oldest major league player was Satchel Paige, who played for the American League's Kansas City A's in September 1965. He was 59 years 80 days old.
- Eddie Gaedel stood 3 feet 7 inches and weighed 65 pounds. He pinch-hit for the St. Louis Browns on August 19, 1951, in a game against the Detroit Tigers. His jersey was numbered 1/8 and Gaedel was qualified as the shortest major league ball player.

## Anniversary Celebrated

- "Casey at the Bat" is a baseball classic. It is a poem written about a mighty baseball hero who failed in the clutch of a very serious game. It was written by Ernest L. Thayer when he was a 25-year-old graduate from Harvard. It was first published on June 3, 1888. Thayer was paid $5 for his poem. On May 18,1888, at Wallack's Theater in New York City, it was first recited by William De Wolfe Hopper. He later repeated his performance about 10,000 times over the next few years. On May 18, 1988, the poem's 100th anniversary was celebrated.

## Sportly Quotes

- "Baseball, it is said, is only a game. True. And the Grand Canyon is only a hole in Arizona. Not all holes, or games, are created equal."                    – George F. Will (1990)
- "Infield practice is more mystic ritual than preparation, encouraging the big-leaguer, no less than the duffer in the stands, to believe in spite of all evidence to the contrary, that playing ball is a snap."          – Roger Angell (1994)

- "It is an old baseball joke that big-inning baseball is affirmed in the Bible, in Genesis. 'in the big inning, God created...'"
  – George F. Will (1990)
- "I've never heard a crowd boo a homer, but I've heard plenty of boos after a strike-out." – Babe Ruth
- "Baseball is too much of a sport to be called a business, and too much of a business to be called a sport."
  – Phillip K. Wrigley

## Who Were The Spiders?

- The Spiders were a Cleveland team which had the first American Indian to play professional baseball. Louis Sockolexis was a native Maine Indian. After he began playing for the Spiders the name of the team was changed to the Cleveland Indians in honor of Sockolexis.

## What's In A Bat

- In 1884, John "Bud" Hillerich, from Louisville, Kentucky, made the first known custom-made baseball bat. He worked as an apprentice in his father's wood-turning shop. One warm spring day, he sneaked off from the shop to watch the Louisville Eclipse play a few innings. While watching, the team's best hitter, Pete "Old Gladiator" Browning, broke his bat. When the game

was over, Bud offered to make a new bat for Browning. Browning accepted the offer. The two men then went to the Hillerich shop where they selected a sturdy piece of white ash timber. Hillerich placed the timber on the wood lathe and began shaping it into a bat. Browning kept testing the bat until he felt it was just right.

- The next day when the Louisville Eclipse played, Browning made three long hits and gave the credit for his success to his new bat. After the game the entire team went to the Hillerich shop to get their own custom-made bats. The bat business became a huge success, and The Hillerich and Bradsby Company has been making Louisville Slugger professional baseball bats for over one hundred years.
- Ash trees are used to make the Louisville Slugger baseball bat. The ash wood has the strength and flexibility and the lightness in weight needed to make a good bat. It takes forty to sixty years to grow an ash tree that is the right size to make baseball bats. After the trees are cut, they are shipped to the mill yard, where they are inspected and measured. The logs are then cut into forty-inch lengths. The logs are then inspected again. If a log is flawed by knots or if the grain is not straight, the log is set aside and sold for other uses. Only half of the wood cut from the forest actually ends up as Louisville Slugger bats. The logs are now split into six to eight pieces from which billets are made. They then go to a lathe to take off the rough edges. The billets are then divided into two groups, one which will be used as the hand-made professional bats and the other for the machine-made non-professional bats. From here the billets are strapped together into bundles and shipped across the Ohio River to Slugger Park in Jeffersonville, Indiana. It is here that the billets go through the seasoning process, which may take from six months to two years, depending on how much moisture is in the wood. It is after this drying-out process that the billets are then finished into the Louisville Slugger baseball bats.

## A Most Unusual Bat

- In the 1920's Heinie Groh played third base for the New York Giants. When it was his turn to bat, he used a bat shaped like a wine bottle.

## A Very Unusual Home Plate

- Cliff Carroll was a professional baseball player in the late 1800's. Carroll always brought his pet monkey with him to every game. When Carroll's pet caught a cold and died, the Pittsburgh team felt so bad that they held a special ceremony for the little creature and buried him under home plate.

## What Makes A Baseball Curve?

- It has been demonstrated with the use of cameras that a baseball may curve as much as 6 1/2 inches from its normal path. This phenomenon is caused by "the Bernoulli effect". The Bernoulli effect is a rather complicated scientific law developed by a man called Bernoulli. Bernoulli pointed out that there are two kinds of pressure in a fluid, such as air or water. One is dynamic and the other is static. The dynamic pressure is created when a moving fluid, such as air, comes into contact with an object. On the other hand, static pressure is the pressure existing within the fluid itself, the pressure of one atom against another. The Bernoulli effect states that the static pressure goes down as the speed goes up.

- When a ball is thrown by a pitcher, he makes the ball spin as it leaves his hand. As the ball spins, it carries air around with it by friction. The air passing the ball and the air spinning around the ball are going in the same direction on one side. On the other side, the air spinning around the ball is going in the opposite direction to the motion of the air past the ball. The ball then moves toward the side where there is lower static pressure, therefore making the ball curve.

## You're Never Too Old

- The Kids and the Kubs are two teams that comprise the Three Quarter Century Softball Club, Inc., of St. Petersburg, Florida. The qualifications to be a member of either team are strong legs and a keen eye. Even more important, you have to be at least seventy-five years old. The two teams battle it out three times a week from November through March. The players on the team include Jim Waldie, who is eighty-eight and plays left field for the Kids. He bats consistently over .400 and is able to nail runners with his incredible throwing arm. Bill Davis is a triple threat as he is a catcher, a pitcher and a second baseman. He is a mere ninety-one. One of the youngest players in the club is Ed Stauffer. He is seventy-six years old and used to play for the St. Louis Browns. Stauffer has been barred from the mound after pitching a shutout. He has also been the leader in hitting, with an .835 batting average, and has made a total of 30 home runs.

# CURIOUS PHENOMENA
by V. B. Darrington

## Athletes In Action

- Huge crowds attend American sporting events. Crowds of around 100,000 are common at major events like the Super Bowl. But those crowds must seem small to the Brazilians. Every January 1 in Sao Paulo, Brazil, hordes of spectators line the roads of the city to cheer on the contestants in a foot race. The race is a little over five miles long. But squeezed along those five miles of roads are over one million people.
- On May 4, 1975, Bob Watson of the Houston Astros baseball team scored a run. But it wasn't just another run. It was run number one million for major league baseball. It took the cumulative scoring efforts of all major league players 99 years to score all those runs.
- The most successfully prolific heavyweight champion boxer was Rocky Marciano. He had 49 fights as champion and won them all. Of those 49 fights, 43 he won by knock-outs.

## Sleeping Policemen

- Drivers in Jamaica are not surprised to see sleeping policemen. In fact, the highway signs even warn motorists to look out for sleeping policemen. As drivers approach a sleeping policeman, they simply slow down, and drive right over the top of it. That's because a "sleeping policeman" is just a speed bump in the road.

## Got Milk?

- Most people think of powdered milk as something very modern. But 700 years ago desert soldiers made powdered milk by drying horse's milk in the sun. The dried milk was thereby reserved for very long periods of time without refrigeration. When the soldiers wanted to use the milk, they just mixed the powder with water.

## Fit For A King

- King Hussein, the ruler of Jordan, was fond of his three large palaces. But the King found it time-consuming and impractical to walk around the palaces. Hussein solved the problem by using a mini bike to carry him from one point to another down the long, spacious hallways.

## "Money To Burn"

- A Japanese man named Yokio Yazaki wasn't rich. But he had saved a considerable sum of money and wanted a good, safe place to hide it. He secretly put the money in a toaster oven in his kitchen. Everything was fine until his wife decided to make some toast. Poor Yazaki found out the hard way what it's like to have "money to burn."

## Phonebook Phenomena

- There are an awfully lot of telephones in Manhattan. In fact, to make a year's supply of Manhattan phone books takes the paper made from 43,000 trees, 100,000 pounds of ink, and 35,375 pounds of glue. In a single year, almost a million and a half Manhattan phone books are made. If they were all stacked on top of one another, the stack would reach a height of 40 miles.

## Men With Vision

- In 1911, a man named Hugo Gernsback wrote down his version of what he foresaw in the future. Many of Gernsback's most outrageous predictions have come true. For example, he said man would travel in space. He also said plastics, tape recorders, and fluorescent lights would be invented. He said people would use radar to help them travel in airplanes and ships. And he said that people would watch TV on small sets that could be held up to the eyes like binoculars. However, Gernsback predicted many things that haven't panned out— at least not yet. He predicted that people would take vacations on the moon. He said people would live in cities that float in the air.

- The first motor boat was invented by James Rumsey. He piloted it up the Potomac River in 1784. One of those watching was George Washington.
- A man in Belgium named Camille Genatsy invented an electric automobile. The car was remarkable in that it could travel at speeds up to 65 miles an hour. The car was also remarkable in that Genatsy invented the car in 1899.
- In 1939 a man named Igor Sikorsky invented and flew the first helicopter used in the U.S. He called it "Igor's Nightmare." Sikorsky also invented the world's first flying boat and the first airplane that had more than one engine.
- Sikorsky's offspring are still active in designing flying craft. His grandson has recently invented an odd little propeller-driven boat that speeds across the water until it actually becomes airborne. The boat lifts into the air and actually cruises several feet above the water. The craft is extremely safe, and it operates much more cheaply per mile than conventional speedboats do.

## Stick 'Em Up

- Curtis Nasdahl had a very bad day. His troubles began when he decided to rob a bar in New York City. He walked in, pointed a gun at the bar owner, and asked for money. When Nasdahl looked to the side, the bar owner grabbed the gun

So You Think You're Having A Really Bad Day

and threw it to another employee. The employee promptly dropped the gun into the basement through a hole in the floor. Nasdahl pleaded, "Give me back my gun," but by then he had lost his advantage. No one paid any attention to him. Since the jig was up, he ran out of the bar. Just outside the door, he slipped on a patch of ice and fell. At that moment, a policeman walked up and arrested the would-be robber. The policeman had stopped when he noticed the car Nasdahl had driven to the heist. It had been reported stolen, and it had been parked on the wrong side of the street.

- A man entered a hotel in Buffalo, New York, and told the clerk he needed a job. So the clerk wrote down the man's name and address. Then the man pulled out a gun and forced the clerk to open the cash register. He got away with $52. Later, the clerk gave the man's name and address to the police. The police went to that address and arrested the robber.

## Not So Average

- The average pencil can draw a line 35 miles long before it runs out of lead.
- Golf balls have been clocked at speeds up to170 miles per hour.
- The shortest U.S. President was James Madison. He was five-feet-four-inches tall.
- Americans swallow 17 billion aspirin tablets a year. That's an average of 77 aspirins for every person.

## Whale Of A Tale

- No one knows exactly why the humpback whale does what it does. The huge beast will occasionally dive to great depths and then swim rapidly toward the surface. Upon reaching the surface, the 80,000-pound leviathan leaps high into the air, and slams back into the water with tremendous force. Some experts speculate that the whale rids his body of troublesome barnacles and parasites by crashing into the sea. Other scientists firmly believe that the huge animal is just playing.
- The humpback also likes to "sing." It is said that its noises travel hundreds of miles under water. The songs of the

humpback are sold commercially on CD's and cassettes. Many people find the haunting calls of the whale to be relaxing.

- The largest animal ever to live on earth is 100 feet long and weighs 400,000 pounds. It's not a dinosaur. In fact this huge animal is still on the earth. The monster is the remarkable blue whale.

- In order to cross San Francisco's Golden Gate Bridge, a driver must pay a toll. However, if the driver doesn't have the money, he can pawn his way across. The toll collectors are instructed to take virtually any object worth at least as much as the toll. As a result, travelers have paid with an odd collection of "fares" over the years. People have paid their way across the Bridge with golf clubs, watches, bibles, and even Christmas trees. Of course these people can reclaim their property by returning with cash—and most people do return, but about one out of every four people never returns.

## Unusual Animal Facts

- Organic substances from all over the world are used in the traditional practice of Chinese medicine. Rare funguses and plants are ground into mystical powders and potions. Animal parts are also highly prized. The gall-bladder of an American Black bear can easily fetch hundreds of dollars. But the trade in animal parts is not just limited to bears.

- The demand for animal parts has caused a serious poaching problem among many species. The horn of the Java rhino is so valuable that the animal has been hunted nearly into extinction. A mere ounce of the ground horn has been sold for more than $1500. To deter poachers from killing the few rhinos that are left, game officers tranquilize the ferocious animals and cut off the horn.

- Scorpions are among the most ancient creatures in existence. They have changed little during their long stay on earth. Some scorpions are not poisonous, but most pack a syringe of venom in their menacing tail. The scorpion is a hunter, but it has very poor eyesight. Instead it relies on a broom-like structure attached to its belly to guide it over rough terrain and to sense vibrations from nearby prey. When a scorpion finds another insect, it grasps it with its front pincers and injects a paralyzing poison into its victim through the sharp hollow end of its tail. The scorpion then eats its prey alive. The largest scorpions can be larger than 8 inches. In an unusual twist of convention, these heavyweights are even known to hunt mice and other small mammals.

- In Arkansas in 1974, an entire flock of ducks fell from the sky. Local people were amazed to see the ducks scattered across the ground, and they were even more surprised that the ducks were frozen. Scientists could only surmise that the whole flock of ducks had frozen to death when they flew through a mass of very cold air.

- In the dark forests of Java, researchers have discovered a species of huge skunks. The animals have been compared in size to German shepherd dogs.

- In January of 1978, a female deer was captured in Wyoming. The deer was unusual in that it had antlers. Usually, only the male mule deer sprouts horns.

- Because of the crowded conditions in Japan there is little room for large pets like dogs and cats. Japanese people compensate by adopting insects as pets instead. Some people pay as much as $3 for a grasshopper, a beetle, or a cricket. One Japanese store reportedly sold $10,000 worth of bugs in a month.

- In order for one bee to make one tablespoon of honey, it must make 4,200 trips to flowers. Bees actually fly so much that they eventually wear their wings to a tattered frazzle.

- Crocodiles of the Nile have a dental plan. The crocodiles in Egypt's Nile River have a unique way to keep tooth problems away. After it finishes eating, a crocodile holds its long, many-toothed mouth wide open. Then along comes a bird called a plover. The bird walks around the crocodile's mouth picking debris from between the crocodile's teeth. This works out well for both animals. The plover gets its fill of tasty morsels to eat. And the crocodile gets clean teeth.
- Twenty newborn opossums can fit into a tablespoon.
- Ukulele means "jumping fleas" in the Hawaiian language.

## Long Pigs?

- The inhabitants of the large island of New Guinea have lived in isolation until modern times. They are known for their head hunting and cannibalism. Sailors in the past commented on the odd way the natives had of referring to them as "long pigs." Little did the sailors know that the natives were actually sizing them up as a meal. "Long pig" is what the natives called their human entrees.

# TIDBITS ODDSNENNZ

by J.C. Walker

## But How Was He At Checkers?

- Former President Richard Nixon may have had his flaws, but apparently one of his assets was that he knew the game of poker inside and out. He learned to play as a teenager working in a traveling carnival show, and while seeming to play a conservative game, he rarely lost. During a hot poker night during World War II, Nixon bluffed a commanding officer out of $1500 with a pair of deuces.
- "It took me fifteen years to discover that I had no talent for writing, but I couldn't give it up, because by that time, I was too famous." – Robert Benchley

## Elementary

- Forget Madonna, forget Julio Iglesias, forget any other pop idols you may have heard about recently – the biggest fan club in the world honors an erudite, prudish, drug-addicted Victorian-era violinist who never existed. Proponents around the world apparently do believe that Sherlock Holmes, master detective, and his confidant and sometime roommate, Dr. Watson, were real people, and that Arthur Conan Doyle simply was an agent selling memoirs of their deductive adventures. These fans collect the stories about Holmes and Watson that have accumulated over the years, and always refer to them as "The Sacred Writings." The tomes have been produced in Bengali, Catlan, Chinese, Korean, Icelandic, Dutch, Gaelic, Finnish, French, Malaysian, German, Hebrew,

Hungarian, Spanish, Italian and Japanese, while other treasures such as Sherlock cookbooks, joke books, salt and pepper shakers, Christmas tree ornaments, nesting dolls, and exposes by nemesis Professor Moriarty are also available. Devotees write poetry to the Master which they share on the Internet and at special Sherlock conventions, at which they also are likely to all show up in 19th century clothing. At home, individuals band together in clubs that take their names from locations and people in Doyle's books. Ultimate homage is paid when a fan travels from the other side of the globe to visit Reichenbach Fall in Europe, where Holmes and the evil Moriarty, locked in combat, met their untimely ends.

- "The trouble with unemployment is that the minute you wake up in the morning you're on the job."     – Slappy White

## State Secret

- Don't fall asleep on that bus tour of New England or you'll miss Vermont. The French originally discovered the area and settled it in 1609, obviously during the summer months, because they named it Verdes Montagnes – The Green Mountains. The name was continually simplified over the years, to Verd Mont and eventually, Vermont. The state is still so tiny and sparsely populated it has one congressional seat, occupied by the House of Representative's only congressman who is neither a Democrat nor a Republican, Independent Bernard Sanders.

- "I went to a wedding...I couldn't believe the groom was married in rented shoes. You're making a commitment for a lifetime, and your shoes have to be back by five-thirty. I was the best man at the wedding...if I'm the best man, why is she marrying him?" – Jerry Seinfeld

## Read On

- David Eugene Ray of Franklin, Tennessee, recently decided he'd had enough of not being able to read and enrolled in literacy classes. He celebrated his 99th birthday just before graduation.
- "My brain is the key that sets me free."

– Harry Houdini, Escape Artist

## It's In The Details

- Lt. Colonel George Armstrong Custer was a well-known headache to the U.S. Army long before that Battle of Little Big Horn unpleasantness which brought them so much bad press. Historians have long been bemused that no one seemed to notice before then that he graduated last in his class at West Point in 1861 and was temporarily suspended for executing Army deserters – they'd had enough of a forced march across Kansas because he was homesick and wanted to see his wife.
- "Why do they call it rush hour when nothing moves?"

– Robin Williams

- "Television – a medium, so called because it is neither rare nor well done." – Ernie Kovacs

## Always Be Careful What You Put In Writing

- There has to be irony somewhere in the story about the handwritten page of George Washington's inaugural speech rough draft of 1789 which he designed as a concluding section but never used. It's full of florid 18th Century references to slavery, to the tyranny of kings and the imperative of people governing themselves in the new land – yet the page was discovered in an album stored in a decaying box under a sofa in a town 85 miles outside London, England. Sold at a London auction house in June of 1996, the piece was a rough draft that the Father of Our Country wisely never used. Apparently his heirs gave it to Jared Sparks, later president of Harvard College, who then gave it as a souvenir to British geologist Sir Charles Lyell when he visited the United States in 1841. The sofa and the house that were the eventual repository of the inaugural page belonged to a Lyell descendent, whose death prompted the visit by the auction house personnel who made the discovery.

- "I took the vacation I wanted all my life. I packed Alice and the kids and all the luggage in our station wagon and headed it right straight to Canada. Then I went to Las Vegas and had a ball." – George Gobel

## Boop Is A Boop Is A Boop

- If you've searched in vain for the perfect gift for the videophile who seems to have everything, your troubles are over. Republic Pictures recently released "Betty Boop: The Definitive Collection" in an eight-volume boxed set that includes 115 of Max and Dave Fleischer's Depression-era cartoons and the essential companion booklet, "Betty Boop Boopliography." Miss Boop originally achieved stardom after having been introduced as a walk-on friend to her dog Bimbo, with the winking, wiggling bombshell quickly stealing the show. Bimbo faded as the brunette star's innuendo and curves also brought the notoriety which helped inspire Hollywood's straight-laced Production Code censorship in the late 1930's. Yet to know Betty was to love her – among the Boopster's devoted fans at that time were Gertrude Stein and Jean-Paul Sartre.

- "Our bombs are incredibly smart. In fact, our bombs are better educated than the average high school graduate. At least they can find Kuwait." – A. Whitney Brown

## Song Titles We'll Never Forget

- "She Was Bred in Old Kentucky But She's Only a Crumb Up Here."  – Curly Howard
- "I'm So Miserable Without You It's Almost Like Having You Around."  – Kip Addotta
- "He Didn't Like Her Apartment So He Knocked Her Flat."  – Homer Haynes
- "Your Eyes Match Garbo's, Baby, I Wish They Matched Each Other." – Henry Morgan
- "I Got Tears in My Ears From Lying on My Back While Crying Over You."  – Homer and Jethro
- "What gets me is that estimated tax return. You have to guess how much you're gonna make. You have to fill it out, fix it up, sign it, send it in. I sent mine in last week. I didn't sign it. If I have to guess how much I'm gonna make, let them guess who sent it." – Jimmy Edmondson (Professor Backwards)

## Too Young To Retire

- The recycling industry is excited about a new product that reuses old tires and keeps kids safe. A French company – which recycles 3 million tires a year – is developing a process that grinds up the old tread, then adds a secret ingredient and mixes it together in a cement mixer. Three minutes later, the goo is poured onto a playground surface, just like asphalt. Voila–a cut-and-scrape-free play surface.
- "A fellow told me he was going to hang-glider school. He said, "I've been going for three months." I said, "How many successful jumps do you need to make before you graduate?" He said, "All of them."

     – Red Skelton

## Massive

- Obscure big stuff you never in your wildest dreams ever thought might actually exist:
- The world's largest flying paper airplane made its only flight on May 16, 1995, at the Faculty of Aerospace Engineering at Delft University of Technology in the Netherlands. Built (if that's the word) by students, the plane had a wingspan of 45 feet 10 inches, and flew a distance of 114 feet 2 inches.
- The largest painting in the world pays homage to none other than Elvis Presley. The King fills a space totalling 76,726 square feet, and he was created by students of Savannah College of Art and Design and members of the local community in Tybee Island, Georgia, on April 8, 1995.
- The longest dragon in history measured 5,550 feet long, and required 610 people inside to prance about to make it appear to be dancing at the Temple of Heaven in Beijing, China, on May 19, 1995.
- "People down South are incredibly polite. Even their war was civil." – Dudley Moore

## It's So Crazy It Just Mite Work

- It's no joke that beekeepers in the United States are having a serious infestation problem in the hives, with tiny red mites obliterating bees in numbers that threaten national honey production and pollination of many crops. One father and son team in Washington, however, believe they've found the solution – they call it "aromatherapy for bees." The pair mix up huge batches of cake frosting and wintergreen oil and place slabs of the stuff in the center of afflicted hives. The bees go crazy, of course, swarming around the sweet antidote, and the mites die as soon as they feed on the bees' blood, which is full of wintergreen oil.

## Here's The Poop

- It's the little things that count – just ask any new parent – but the power of one can make something that seems insignificant important. If the 32 million moms and dads in the U.S. would use only one less disposable diaper every 24 hours, there would be 32 million less in our garbage and landfills each day. The mind boggles at the impact for the environment when that figure is multiplied by 365 days a year.

- "When you're dating you're so insecure. My last relationship, I was always there for her and she dumped me. I told her about it. I said, 'Remember when your grandma died? I was there. Remember when you flunked out of school? I was there. Remember when you lost your job? I was there.' She said, 'I know – you're bad luck.'" – Tom Arnold

# VALENTINE'S DAY
by Kathy Wolfe

## First Quote To Note

- "Say it with flowers, Say it with sweets; Say it with kisses, Say it with eats; Say it with jewelry, Say it with drink. But always be careful not to say it with ink." – Anonymous

## Early Holidays

- There were probably two men considered to be St. Valentine, and both were supposedly beheaded on Feb. 14. The more commonly accepted legend names St. Valentine as a priest in early Rome, around the year 260. The Roman emperor at that time forbade his soldiers to marry because he believed that single men made better soldiers. In the name of love and in defiance of the emperor's edict, St. Valentine secretly married couples.

- Tradition places the first Valentine letter around 1415, when a Frenchman, the Duke of Orleans, was captured in battle and put in an English prison. From there on Valentine's Day, he composed rhymed love letters to his wife.

- In England during the 1700's, women wrote men's names on little bits of paper, then encased the papers in pieces of clay, and dropped all the clay pieces into the water. The first paper to rise to the top, according to legend, was the name of the woman's true love.

- Some unmarried women in the 1700's pinned five bay leaves to their pillow on Feb. 13. That night, they supposedly dreamt of their future husbands. Perhaps this is where we derive the expression "the man of my dreams."

- An old Valentine custom had men write women's names on bits of paper to be placed in a jar. The name which was drawn was the man's "Valentine," and he spent the day paying special attention to her, including gifts, often a pair of gloves. Some of these men pinned the lady's name to their shirt sleeve and wore it for several days. This could well be where the phrase "wearing his heart on his sleeve" originated.

- In Victorian days, a young woman used her fan to convey a secret message to her beau. Drawing her fan across the cheek meant "I love you," while if she twirled it in her right hand, she was warning him, "We are being watched."

- The first person to manufacture Valentines commercially was Esther Howland in 1847. She soon built her business into $100,000 annually.

- In the late 1800's, humorous Valentines with derogatory verse called "penny dreadfuls" could be purchased for a penny if there was someone you wanted to insult.

- Cupid, Roman mythology's god of love, is said to have had two different images, good and bad. The good, of course, depicts him as a happy chubby infant with wings who unites lovers. He causes his "victims" to fall in love with one shot of his trusty bow and arrow. However, mythology also describes him as a tall, handsome young man, but a cruel husband to his beautiful wife, the princess Psyche, whom he refused to allow sight of him. He would allow her to be with him only in the dark. One night in desperation, Psyche lit a lamp to gaze upon his face while he was asleep, which caused Cupid to desert her.

# Sweets For The Sweet

- Thinking about chocolates for your sweetie? You'll be glad to know that chocolate ranks high in food value and contains several vitamins and minerals. It was also the belief of the Aztec Indians that eating the cacao bean was a source of wisdom and knowledge because the seeds had been brought to their land from Paradise.

- About 4 billion pounds of candy are purchased by Americans each year, about 19 lbs. per person on the average. Our Canadian friends average only 17 lbs. per person.

- Egyptians were the first candymakers, 3,000 years ago, when they mixed fruits and nuts with honey.

- For 68 years, the Hershey Chocolate Company operated with no advertising budget. It did not advertise its product until July of 1970.

- Before it is molded into bars, milk chocolate is stirred by machines for 72 hours to achieve the smoothest chocolate possible.

- If you plan to give your sweetheart perfume for Valentine's Day, you might want to know that one of the ingredients in many perfumes is coal tar. And in order to prolong the fragrance, manufacturers add substances taken from beavers, male musk deer, and sperm whales. Still other ingredients are derived from turpentine.

- You should also know that most perfumes are produced synthetically using chemical substances, and even the best perfumes contain only about 10% flower petal oil dissolved in alcohol.

- It takes ten million jasmine flowers to produce only 2.2 lbs. of the fragrant oil.

- Although a perfume may smell like one specific fragrance, such as the rose, it can actually be a blend of up to 500 ingredients.

- If your Valentine asks that you give her a Pascali, a Chrysler Imperial, a Rubaiyat, a Floradora, a Montezuma, or an

Iceberg, she's asking for a rose from the list of the more popular varieties.

- In the 1600's, perfume was made by placing rose petals in white wine, adding fragrant herbs and spices, and allowing the mixture to ferment for two weeks.
- Can you identify the person who made the popular quote, "A rose by any other name would smell as sweet?" It was playwright William Shakespeare.
- All states in the Union have state flowers, but the national flower for the U.S. is the rose.

## Love And Marriage

- "Love may make the world go round, but it doesn't pay for the ride." – Anonymous
- Courtship during Victorian times had definite rules of etiquette, and, according to one authority of those times, the lady "is not to allow the young gentleman to kiss you until he has proposed marriage." Of course, there were those who disagreed, such as the expert who advised that "the prudent maiden should not allow her lover to kiss her even after their engagement. Not until after marriage should such a favor be granted."
- Romeo and Juliet were two young lovers caught in the middle of a long-standing feud between their families, the Montagues and the Capulets. They were secretly married only one day after they met. But the feud would not allow them wedded bliss. Under pressure from her father to marry her cousin, Juliet planned her escape, and a friendly friar administered a drug that put her into a deep temporary sleep, resembling death. Romeo believed her dead and poisoned himself. When Juliet awoke and found Romeo dead, she stabbed herself. Romeo's last words were, "Thus with a kiss I die." So the one bright spot in this sad story? The families agreed to end their feud as a result of the deaths.
- It was Sir Alfred Tennyson who said, "'Tis better to have loved and lost than never to have loved at all."

- "Love is patient, love is kind...it is not easily angered, it keeps no record of wrongs. Love never fails." – I Cor. 13
- Minnie Pearl had these thoughts on marriage, "Gettin' married's a lot like getting into a tub of hot water. After you get used to it, it ain't so hot."
- Lovebirds are actually part of the parrot family and are named so because of their caresses of each other with their bills, showing great affection for each other. Their original home is Africa.
- The oldest man to tie the knot was Harry Stevens, who married his 84-year-old bride when he was 103, at a retirement home in Wisconsin.
- "To keep your marriage brimming with love in a loving cup, whenever you're wrong admit it; whenever you're right, shut up." – Ogden Nash.
- A little girl had been told the story of "Snow White" at pre-school one day and hurried home to relate the story to her mother. Bit by bit, she shared the tale with Mommy and was at the point of Prince Charming is bringing Snow White back to life with a kiss when she stopped and asked, "Do you know what happened then?" Mommy, familiar with the story, said, "Yes, they lived happily ever after," to which the little girl replied dismally, "No, they got married."
- The fourth finger of the left hand became the "ring finger" for wedding rings because of a tradition that a delicate nerve ran from that finger to the heart.
- One woman expressed her love for her man in a recently-seen bumper sticker: "All men are idiots, and I married their king."
- "My wife and I were happy for twenty years. Then we met."
  – Rodney Dangerfield
- The longest marriage on record is 86 years.
- The most-married person is Scotty Wolfe, who has been married 27 times, one wife at a time, with the first nuptials taken in 1927. He thinks he had 41 children.

- The King of Siam portrayed in the film "The King and I" reportedly had 9,000 wives, but not monogamously.
- "Love covers a multitude of sins." – The Apostle Peter
- The son of a sheik in the Middle East married a princess in 1981 in a wedding that lasted seven days, had 20,000 guests, and holds the record for being the most expensive, $44 million.
- The throwing of rice at weddings represents a wish for children and a long life for the couple, since rice, according to tradition, is the symbol of fertility and longevity.
- "From birth to 18, a girl needs good parents. From 18 to 35, she needs good looks. From 35 to 55, she needs a good personality. From 55 on, she needs good cash!" – Sophie Tucker
- "What we love we shall grow to resemble."

  – Bernard of Clairvaux
- One couple in Mexico City believed in long engagements. After being engaged for 67 years, they finally wed at age 82.
- "I believe a little imcompatibility is the spice of life, particularly if he has income and she is pattable." – Ogden Nash
- Unfortunately, Ida and Simon Stern, a Wisconsin couple, decided they'd had enough of marriage and divorced in 1984. Ida was 91 and Simon was 97.
- Research has shown that marital strife can weaken the immune system and cause physical illness. Those couples that show hostility toward each other have reduced levels of key immune system cells.
- "Love is a rocky trail, but it promises a scenic ride." – G. Montana
- All in the name of love, King Edward VIII of England gave up his throne to marry Wallis Simpson, an American divorcee. The English government refused to accept her as queen because of her two divorces. His successor was his brother George, the father of Queen Elizabeth.
- "Take it from me, marriage isn't a word — it's a sentence."

  – King Vidor
- Not every Hollywood marriage is doomed to fail. Bob Hope has been married 62 years, James Cagney was married 63

years, and Charlton Heston, 52 years so far. However, one of Patty Duke's marriages lasted only 13 days.

- "Married men live longer than single men. But married men are a lot more willing to die." – Johnny Carson

## Massacre

- The St. Valentine's Day Massacre took place on Feb. 14, 1929, in Chicago. Al Capone's mobster gang was held responsible for dressing as policemen and gunning down seven members of the rival Bugs Moran gang. They were never convicted. Capone was the most powerful gangster in Chicago, and controlled bootlegging, gambling, and prostitution rings.
- "Scarface" Capone claimed the scar on his left cheek was the result of a World War I injury. In actuality, he never served in the war. He served as a bouncer in a Brooklyn saloon, where he was involved in a knife fight over a woman.
- The only charge Al Capone was ever jailed on was income tax evasion. Elliot Ness was the FBI agent instrumental in locking him up. Capone spent eight years in prison. He died of syphilis at age 48.

## Final Bit

- Man: "Would you still love me if I lost all my money? Woman: "Yes, but I'd miss you."

# OUTLAWS AND GUNFIGHTERS
By Mona McKown

### The Polite Outlaw

- A very unconventional outlaw named Charles E. Boles worked the Sierra Nevada foothills and the California Sonoma Coast. He was not the typical cowboy outlaw. He worked alone, walking everywhere he went because of his hate for horses, and he wore a derby instead of a Stetson. He robbed about twenty-nine stagecoaches between 1875 and 1883. He

was better known as "Black Bart." His first robbery was of a Wells Fargo stagecoach, on July 26, 1875. John Shine was the driver of that stagecoach and was duped by "Black Bart." Shine was traveling between Shasta and Fort Ross when suddenly Bart appeared on the road in front of the stagecoach, wearing a flour sack over his head. He was pointing a twelve-gauge directly at Shine. Bart asked Shine, very politely, to throw the strongbox down from the stage. When Shine hesitated, Bart yelled toward the bushes that if Shine tried to get off a shot, he would be loaded with lead. When the driver looked around, he noticed six rifles poking out of the chaparral, aimed directly at him. At that point, Shine decided he had better give the robber what he wanted. Bart opened the strongbox, took out its contents, and hurried off into the bushes, leaving Shine sitting on the stage with the six rifles still aimed at him. After sitting nervously for about fifteen minutes, Shine began to wonder what was going on. He climbed down off the coach, expecting to be killed, but nothing happened. Cautiously he approached the rifle nearest him and discovered it was only a wooden pole. He then checked the others and found the same thing. He then realized that he had been robbed by a lone gunman. Bart was finally arrested on November 3, 1883. He was convicted of only one robbery and was sentenced to ten years in San Quentin. He was released on January 21, 1888, for good behavior. Bart immediately went to Vancouver, British Columbia, and boarded the Empress of China which was going to Japan. He was never heard of again.

## Well-Known Outlaw Families

- The Reno Brothers of Indiana included Frank, John, Simeon, Clinton and William. After the Civil War, they organized all the small outlaw gangs into one big gang and controlled much of the southern Indiana countryside. They were notorious train robbers. Their largest robbery was committed on May 22, 1868, when they held up a Jefferson, Missouri, and Indianapolis train. They were able to obtain $96,000 worth of loot.

- Myra Belle Shirley was born February 5, 1848, in Missouri. Her family moved to Texas after the Kansas-Missouri border war broke out. It was in Texas that she met Cole Younger of the James Gang. She fell in love and had a daughter by him named Pearl. Next she met Jim Reed, who was also an outlaw. She also fell for Reed and bore his son, Edward. In 1869, Belle and Jim, along with two other outlaws, stole $30,000 in gold. After Jim Reed was killed, Belle left her children with her mother and began her full-time career of stealing horses. When she met Sam Starr, a Cherokee Indian, she married him and settled on a piece of land which she called Younger's Bend. Belle Starr continued her career until 1889 when she was killed by a bushwacker.

- Oklahoma was the home of the Dalton brothers. They were cousins of the Younger brothers. There were fifteen children in the Dalton household, but three of them, Bob, Grat, and Emmett rode together as outlaws. Bill, one of their other brothers, became an outlaw later. Their robbing days lasted only eighteen months. Bob and Grat were killed in Coffeyville, on the border of Oklahoma and Kansas, when they tried an unsuccessful raid. Emmett was wounded but recovered. He was sentenced to a life term in the Kansas State Penitentiary, but in 1907 was pardoned and released. He settled in Los Angeles and married his long-time sweetheart, Julia Johnson. He became a building contractor, real estate man and movie writer and was the first to admit that crime does not pay.

## Legend Or Reality

- Was Billy the Kid really a deadly killer, skilled in the use of a six-shooter, or was he a totally different man? The legend built in the American southwestern frontier showed Billy the Kid to be a person who protected the oppressed ranchers against the contemptible cattle barons. However, official documents in government depositories reveal a totally different individual. Billy was actually a lonely, disturbed young man but was honest and loyal to his friends. He was dedicated to his beliefs and was betrayed by the ambitious and corrupt politicians of that time. These documents also wash away the myth that Billy killed a man for every year of his life. Actually, the total is closer to four, some of which were in self-defense and others while he was a member of a vigilante organization.

- Billy the Kid was born Henry McCarty, in New York City. He was one of two sons born to Michael and Catharine McCarty. His father died when Henry was a small child. After his father's death, Henry's mother moved her family west. She has been portrayed as a grieving widow, barely scraping out an existence for herself and her family. This version is quite untrue. Catharine was actually a very successful businesswoman dealing in real estate, hotel operations, laundries, and other services needed by the western communities. Henry and his younger brother, Joseph, helped with the laundry service. Henry was twelve at the time, living in Wichita on the Kansas frontier. In the spring of 1871 Mrs. McCarty became ill, diagnosed with tuberculosis, for which there was no cure. She sold her businesses, moving from Wichita to Denver to New Orleans to Silver City, New Mexico.

- William Henry Antrim had been courting Catharine for the past six years, moving with Catharine and her boys. In 1873, when Henry was fourteen, Antrim married Catharine. When she became bed-ridden, Henry was always at his mother's side, helping in her care. Within four months his mother died. The death of Catharine changed Billy. The once sweet, smiling youngster turned to poker chips and monte. Antrim tried to keep his family together, but Billy was more and more uncontrollable. Billy moved out to work in a family friend's hotel, the Star Hotel in Silver City, run by the Truesdells. The Truesdells' son, Chauncey, was Billy's best friend. Billy worked there for a year and was one of the few employees who never stole anything while working there.

- In August, 1877, Billy killed his first man. Unfortunately, the *Arizona Daily Citizen* did not print the whole story. It did not mention that the deceased man, E. P. Cahill (Windy), was a big bullying-type blacksmith who had repeatedly humiliated and beaten the slim, fair haired, blue-eyed boy then sixteen years of age. After the shooting Billy raced for the door, jumped on a near-by horse and rode out of town. The coroner's jury's verdict called the killing "criminal and unjustifiable and Henry Antrim, alias Kid, is guilty thereof." Thus started the legend of Billy the Kid.

## Stolen Quotes

- "A thief passes for a gentleman when stealing has made him rich." – Thomas Fuller, M.D. (1732)
- "Old burglars never die, they just steal away."
  – Glen Gilbreath (1958)
- "The fact of the matter is that poor men do not often steal, and when they do, it is petty theft, something to eat or perhaps an item of clothing to keep them from the cold. Thieves are usually those who have something and want more."
  – Louis L'Amour (1989)
- "The real reason why Robin Hood robbed only the rich was that the poor had no money." – Anonymous
- "Thieves respect property; they merely wish the property to become their property that they may more perfectly respect it." – G. K. Chesterton (1908)

## The Hole In The Wall Gang

- In the 1890's, this gang was the largest and most organized of all outlaw gangs, although they were not always successful in their robberies. Its most famous members were Butch Cassidy, Kid Curry, the Sundance Kid, and lady outlaw Etta Place, who was Butch Cassidy's common-law wife. Their gang was also known as The Wild Bunch. The group was always impeccably dressed and gave the appearance of being mild-mannered businessmen. The leader of The Wild Bunch was Robert Leroy Parker, alias Butch Cassidy. The most dangerous member of The Hole in the Wall Gang was Harvey Logan, alias Kid Curry. He was of medium height with melancholy dark eyes and usually dressed in a blue suit and wing collar. Lawmen gave him credit for killing fifteen men. His suppressed violence and fast gun made him a figure who was very hard to forget. Kid Curry's reputation as a badman and killer was one which made him feel very proud. Logan always had a large group of beautiful women around him. Even while he was incarcerated in Knoxville, in the Texas frontier, he had women flocking to his cell with flowers, delicious meals and fine presents.

- At a bank in Belle Fourche, South Dakota, the Gang was able to make off with $30,000. In 1899, after splitting up for a while until things cooled down, The Hole in the Wall Gang stopped the Union Pacific's <u>Overland Limited</u> and got away with another $30,000.

- On July 3, 1901, The Hole in the Wall Gang blew up the express car of the <u>Great Northern</u> and rode off with $65,000. The robbery took place about 200 miles east of Great Falls, Montana, near Wagner, Montana. Unfortunately, the currency taken was made up of all new bills and not one of them had as yet been officially signed by the bank. They were worthless. It was shortly after this unsuccessful raid that Butch Cassidy decided it was probably time to leave the country. However, it was another eight years and several more robberies later before Butch Cassidy and the Sundance Kid went to Bolivia. Butch had tried to convince Kid Curry to join them, but Curry refused to go.

## Modern-Day Outlaws

- A Fergus, Ontario, native was caught by police for stealing. The fact that he was caught does not make him so unusual, but what he stole does. He was busted for stealing four and a half quarts of bull semen. While visiting with reporters he said, "I am not what they call a kinky."

- As reported by the Times of London, when the offices of Games and Puzzles, a British publication, was ransacked by thieves it was noted that they made off with several hundred thousand pounds of hard, cold cash. Did the thieves realize that they had made off with "Monopoly" money? Only they know for sure.

- On August 7, 1975, "a very nervous" young man entered a restaurant in Newport, Rhode Island. John Anthony Gibbs demanded that the restaurant's cash be handed over to him, after he waved a gun around in the air. He received $400, put the money into a sack, and attempted to stuff the sack into his shirt pocket. Unfortunately for him, he was also holding his gun with the same hand. The gun discharged under his chin and killed him instantly.

## The Last Look

- Sam Bass was born near Mitchell, Indiana, in 1851. About 1870, he moved to Texas, where he was a cowboy, a mill hand and a deputy sheriff. He remained a deputy until 1875, after which he became an outlaw. He formed a gang, in the Black Hills town of Deadwood, South Dakota, whose purpose was to rob stagecoaches. In 1877, Bass and his gang robbed a Union Pacific train at Big Springs, Nebraska. They netted about $65,000. Sam Bass was called the "good badman" because he gave a portion of what he stole to the poor, much as in the legend of Robin Hood.

# TIDBITS GOES TO THE MOVIES
By V.B. Darrington

### In The Beginning...

- Liza Minnelli, who is the daughter of Vincent Minnelli and Judy Garland, made her motion picture debut at the tender age of just 2-1/2 years old. She debuted in the film "The Good Old Summertime" (1946).
- Robert Blake starred for several seasons as the cagey detective in "Baretta." Young Blake began his acting career by appearing with the little rascals in the "Our Gang" comedies of the '30s. You might also remember his auspicious bit part in "The Treasure of Sierra Madre" (1948), when he sold Humphrey Bogart the winning lottery ticket.
- Jack Nicholson made his first film appearance in Roger Corman's "The Cry Baby Killer" (1964).

### Sporting Actors

- Abbot's paunchy partner, Lou Costello, was once a boxer.
- Bob Hope was also once a boxer. He fought under the name of Packy East. Perhaps that's how he got his trademark nose.
- Johnny Weissmuller earned his role as Tarzan after having earned Olympic gold. He was the top medalist in 1924 in a swimming event.

### "And The Oscar Goes To–"

- In a rare humorous gesture, the Academy gave Walt Disney an Oscar statue and seven tiny miniature statues for his film "Snow White and The Seven Dwarfs" (1937).
- Walt Disney has collected more Academy Awards than any

140

other single member of the motion picture industry. Including his six special awards, he has won 32 of the trophies.

- Until Tom Hanks repeated the feat, only five actors had won Best Actor Awards on more than one occasion: Marlon Brando ("On the Waterfront" and "The Godfather"); Gary Cooper ("Sergeant York" and "High Noon"); Dustin Hoffman ("Kramer vs. Kramer" and "Rain Man"); Fredric March ("Dr. Jekyll and Mr. Hyde" and "The Best Years of Our Lives"); and Spencer Tracy ("Captains Courageous" and "Boys Town").

- "Ben Hur" (1959) still reigns supreme over other films as the only picture to win eleven Oscars, including Best Picture, Best Director, Best Actor, Best Supporting Actor, Sound, Art Direction, Cinematography, Editing Special Effects, Best Score, and Costumes. Charlton Heston's chariot ride has proven tough to equal.

- "It Happened One Night" (1934), "One Flew Over the Cuckoo's Nest" (1976), and "The Silence of the Lambs" (1991) are in a class by themselves having swept the five most coveted Academy Awards (Best Picture Best Director, Best Screenplay, Best Actor, and Best Actress).

- Even in America, only one Western has ever won the Academy Award for Best Picture. It was "Cimarron" (1931).

- John Ford has made his mark on American cinematography. He is the only director to have achieved four awards for Best Director. He was awarded the honor for the films "The Informer" (1935), "The Grapes of Wrath" (1940), "How

Green Was My Valley" (1941), and "The Quiet Man" (1952).

- Katherine Hepburn leads all other actresses. She owns four Oscars. Hepburn needed nearly fifty years to earn her awards. The films were "Morning Glory" (1933), "Guess Who's Coming to Dinner" (1967), "The Lion in Winter" (1968), and "On Golden Pond" (1981).

- Anthony Quinn's role was short but sweet in his 8-minute performance as Gauguin in "Lust For Life" (1956). His performance is the shortest ever to win an Oscar (Best Supporting Actor).

- Tatum O'Neal was only 9 years old when she played a young confidence trickster in the film "Paper Moon" (1973). Her performance netted her an Academy Award. Of course fans of Shirley Temple will be quick to point out that she received a special award for outstanding contribution to screen entertainment when she was only six years old.

- On the other end of the spectrum, Jessica Tandy was the oldest performer to win an Oscar. At 80 years 8 months, she wooed the judges in her appearance in "Driving Miss Daisy" (1989).

- Hattie McDaniel broke the color barrier in 1939 as the first black Academy Award winner. She played the role of Mammy in "Gone With the Wind." Another 24 years passed before Sidney Portier repeated McDaniel's achievement by winning an Oscar for his performance in "Lilies of the Field" (1963).

- Spencer Tracy had a good laugh, and then returned his 1938 Best Actor award to the Academy. His statue had been mistakenly engraved with the name "Dick Tracy."

- The renowned ventriloquist, Edgar Bergen, didn't get much respect. The Academy awarded an Oscar to his dummy, Charlie McCarthy, for his performance in "The Goldwyn Follies" (1938). Fittingly, the Oscar given to the puppet was made of wood—the only wooden Oscar ever given.

- "Midnight Cowboy" (1969) broke all the rules when it won an Oscar for Best Picture. It is the only X-rated film ever to win the award. The film's rating was later changed to an "R".

- Marlon Brando caused a stir when he refused to appear to receive his Academy Award in 1972. Instead he sent a Native American woman to receive the trophy. It was later discovered that the Apache woman was something of an actress in her own right. She had won a pageant as Miss American Vampire of 1970.

## Famous Room-Mates

- Before moving to Hollywood, Stan Laurel and Charlie Chaplin worked together on the English stage. Laurel was Chaplin's understudy in a number of minor productions. When the two struggling actors moved to the U.S., they became roommates in a boarding house. House rules forbid the boarders to cook in their rooms. But Chaplin and Laurel were not easily discouraged. Chaplin would play the violin loudly to cover up the sound of Laurel frying up food on a hot plate.
- Gene Hackman and Dustin Hoffman were another pair of famous roommates. They shared quarters in New York while getting their feet wet in acting. It is hard to believe that the two mega-stars were once voted least likely to succeed by their classmates at the Playhouse Acting School.

## What If?

- Imagine if Clint Eastwood had played the starring role in "Apocalypse Now." He refused the offer, and Martin Sheen did justice to the classic role.
- Ronald Reagan nearly made a break into the annals of A-movie history. He was the first pick to play the role of Rick in "Casablanca" (1942).
- Marlon Brando might have altered the course of history as well. He was heavily favored to play the title role in "Lawrence of Arabia" (1963).
- Doris Day nearly missed her calling. The young songbird originally wanted to be a dancer. Fortunately for the movie industry, she injured her leg while practicing and decided to give singing a whirl.

- Robert Mitchum once served time in a chain gang.
- Lucille Ball flunked out of her first acting school. Her instructor determined that she was too shy.
- Before he became a movie star, W.C. Fields earned a living as a confidence man. By arrangement with a beach-side vendor, whenever business lagged, Fields would pretend to drown. Another con man would rescue Fields and drag him lifelessly onto the beach. Onlookers would soon gather to see the spectacle. And the concession owner would sell refreshments and snacks to his captive customers. Perhaps this is when the future comedian first coined the cynical phrase, "There's a sucker born every minute."

## "We're Off To See The Wizard–"

- Judy Garland is best known for her part in "The Wizard of Oz" (1939). Judy got the role by accident when 20th Century Fox studio asked too high a price to loan her talents to the film's owner, Metro Goldwyn Mayer (MGM).
- Young Judy Garland was the first person ever to contract with a major studio without having to complete a screen test. The young actress stepped into the harness when she was just 13-years-old.
- Depending on your own personal experience in school, you may or may not be surprised that the Wicked Witch of the West ("Wizard of Oz"), Margaret Hamilton, was once a kindergarten teacher.
- Compared to the modern film juggernauts, "The Wizard of Oz" was a bargain. It cost a trifling $3 million dollars to make.

## Looks Aren't Everything

- It is rumored that Cecil B. DeMille took a liking to Charlton Heston when he noticed that the young actor's nose was broken in the same place as Michaelangelo's Moses had his nose broken. In 1956 Cecil B. DeMille hired the actor for the remake of "The Ten Commandments."
- Humphrey Bogart's slight lisp was actually the result of a war wound. During World War II, the ship he was on was

bombed by German sailors. A splinter from the wooden deck was driven into the future star's upper lip. A damaged nerve resulted in partial facial paralysis—and an unforgettable trademark.

- Fred Astaire barely made the cut as a star. His first screen test was an absolute disaster. The report read, "Can't act, slightly bald, can dance a little."

- Clark Gable's first screen test was also a flop. Jack Warner quipped to a co-executive, "Why do you throw away five hundred dollars of our money on a test for that big ape? Didn't you see those big ears when you talked to him? And those big feet and hands, not to mention that ugly face of his?" Since then many women have had a slightly different opinion of the great actor.

## "Frankly My Dear–"

- At tremendous expense, 1,400 actresses were screen tested for the coveted role of Scarlett O'Hara. The studio spent $92,000 just to locate the right girl. As it turned out, the massive search for a star generated a huge amount of publicity. Budding starlets from coast to coast anticipated the release.

- Bette Davis, Susan Hayward, and Paulette Goddard were among the many actresses who were turned down for the part of Scarlett O'Hara in "Gone With the Wind" (1939).

- Suspiciously, Vivien Leigh, who was eventually awarded the role, arrived at the studio for her screen test on the arm of the producer's brother.

## All For The Cost Of A Ticket–

- "American Graffiti" (1973) cost only $775,000 to film. It went on to earn the amazing sum of $40 million and became a modern film classic.

- Steven Speilberg and George Lucas have cornered the market on successful films. Their productions have netted them more than $100 million in profits.

- "Dick Tracy" may not have been the most memorable movie, but don't blame it on the publicist. They spent over $48 million to hype the film.

- The days of the great "Epic" film are probably over. The cost of producing films has gone too high. For example, "Terminator 2, Judgment Day," was the most expensive film ever at the time of its release. It required an outlay of $104 million. Kevin Costner's "Water World" is rumored to have cost more than $200 million.
- By comparison, "Cleopatra" cost $44 million in 1963, the equivalent of nearly $180 million in 1996 dollars. But back then, for that price, you could buy thousands of "extras," hundreds of ornate costumes, and a slim Elizabeth Taylor.
- For "Cleopatra," the costumer didn't hold back. For Miss Taylor alone, the costume expenses exceeded $200,000.
- The average budget for a film in 1990 was $18.1 million.
- Since great art can't be imitated, the producers of the film "Legal Eagles" brought in $10 million worth of paintings and sculptures to enhance the scenes of the movie.
- Darth Vader's <u>Star Destroyer</u> in "Star Wars" was a special effects masterpiece. It cost $100,000 and sported more than 250,000 portholes.
- When Roman Polanski determined that miniatures and piecemeal sets weren't adequate to give the true effect of a pirate galleon, he commissioned a full-sized replica. The

movie "Pirates" (1986) holds the record for the most expensive single prop. The ship cost over $13 million.

- The highest grossing animated film in the history of the movies is "Snow White and the Seven Dwarfs" (1937).

## The Last Hurrah–

- Sam Warner never got the satisfaction of screening his film "The Jazz Singer" to an audience. He died the day before the premier.

# THE LETTER "R"

By Kathy Wolfe

## "R" Things

- If your child is begging for a Belgian, a Dutch, a Havana, a Palomino, a Rex, or a White Flemish Giant, it's a rabbit she wants. A female rabbit is not the same as a hare. Rabbits are smaller and their ears are shorter than those of hares.
- It is not unusual for a female rabbit to give birth five times a year, with five babies at a time. The largest litter of rabbits ever born was 24, in Nova Scotia, Canada.
- If a rabbit is being chased by an enemy, it can hop up to 18 mph and leap 10 ft.
- The first roller coaster in America was at Coney Island in New York City, debuting in 1884. Some of today's roller coasters boast speeds of 70 mph.
- "Rambo III" has the honor of being one of the most violent movies, with 169 acts of violence per hour. It would be interesting to know if the star of the "Rambo films," Sylvester Stallone, would have achieved the same fame if he'd gone by his real name, Sylvester Labofish.
- The front horn of the black rhinoceros can be as long as 3 ft. The rhino uses the horn to uproot small trees in order to eat the leaves and twigs, and to defend itself.
- If someone calls you a rougue, consider yourself insulted. You're being described as lecherous and without virtue or decency.
- Turn on some Latin music, take small steps in a square pattern

with your knees relaxed, and sway your hips. You'll be dancing the Rhumba, which was brought to the U.S. from Cuba about 1914.

- If you experience pain, burning, headaches, numbness, muscle spasms, or difficulty in swallowing, you have the symptoms of rabies. Rabies destroys the nerve cells of part of the brain. Convulsions usually follow and death is almost always the result. You can contract rabies simply by breathing the air in a cave that is home to a large number of bats. The Latin word <u>rabies</u> translates to "rage" or "fury," probably because of the behavior of those infected. Rabies is also called hydrophobia, meaning "fear of water," because the infected animal's ability to swallow water is affected.

- The raccoon and the panda belong to the same animal group family. A baby raccoon is born without the black-haired mask around its eyes and the black rings on its tail. Raccoons are great scavengers, and if you have one raiding your garbage that you'd like to see gone, try sprinkling the top of your trash cans with Lysol, ammonia, or Tabasco sauce.

- "The raucous ruckus from the ribald rapscallion's rhonchus rattled all over Ragusa" translates to "The harsh, noisy disturbance from the vulgar scoundrel's bronchial tubes' disorder made short, sharp sounds through a city in southeast Sicily."

- Rx is the symbol for a prescription drug and can be traced to the Latin word for recipe.

- Beep! Beep! The roadrunner races down the highway at speeds up to 15 mph. It stands 2 ft. tall, half of which is tail. It also answers to the name of ground cuckoo and chaparral cock.

- If you listened to the radio constantly during 1941, you would have heard the Pepsi-Cola broadcast 296,426 times.

C.WENZEL

- If you're a baby boomer, you may have watched an early TV puppet show, "Rootie Kazootie," which ran from 1950-1952. Other characters included El Squeeko Mouse and Gala Poochie.
- A rainbow is produced by the refraction of sunlight in drops.
- Theodore "Teddy" Roosevelt was the youngest president to take office, at age 42. John Kennedy was the youngest to be ELECTED to the office. Roosevelt took office upon the assassination of President McKinley. The oldest elected was Ronald Reagan, two weeks shy of his 70th birthday. He was re-elected at age 73.
- Teddy Roosevelt holds the record for the highest number of handshakes at an office function — 8,513 on New Year's Day, 1907.
- On Valentine's Day of 1884, Teddy Roosevelt lost both his wife and his mother. His wife died from complications of childbirth two days after the birth of their daughter, and his mother succumbed to typhoid fever. He later lost three of his four sons, who were killed while serving in wars.
- Teddy Roosevelt suffered from insomnia. He found the best cure to be a shot of cognac in a glass of milk.
- In the "Batman" series, Robin is the secret identity of Dick Grayson.
- Virginia McMath danced her way to stardom in such films as "Top Hat," "Flying Down to Rio," and "Shall We Dance?" She became the world's most famous ballroom dancer, along with her partner Fred Astaire. Perhaps you'll recognize her as Ginger Rogers.
- Bhagwan Rajneesh, an Indian guru, incurred the anger of many Oregon residents when he established a commune there. He was deported from the U.S. in 1985, at which time he was the owner of 93 Rolls-Royces.
- The original members of the Rolling Stones were Mick Jagger, Brian Jones, Keith Richard, Charlie Watts, and Bill Wyman. When Bill Wyman was 42, he married 18-year-old

Mandy Smith. Wyman's son then married Mandy Smith's mother; he was 30, she was 46, a marriage that would make Bill Wyman his own grandfather-in-law. Unfortunately, Bill and Mandy divorced after only 17 months.

- The Rolling Stones took their name from a hit song recorded in 1948 by Muddy Waters, "Rolling Stone Blues." The Stones have never won a Grammy Award.

- Andy Rooney gives us sound advice, "Go to bed. Whatever you're staying up late for isn't worth it."

- Poor Richard's Almanac was supposedly written by Richard Saunders. In actuality, the author was Benjamin Franklin.

- If you think that the story of Pocahontas ends with her living happily ever after with handsome John Smith, you'd better check your history book. Pocahontas married John Rolfe, an English settler from Jamestown, VA, who played a large role in developing tobacco as the main crop of Virginia. Rolfe took her to England, where she took the English name Rebecca following her Christian baptism. Unfortunately, Rolfe and Pocahontas enjoyed only three years of wedded bliss, as she died of smallpox in 1617. Rolfe returned to America, where he was killed by Indians five years later.

- Famous humorist Will Rogers started out as a cattle driver in Texas. After a stint at ranching, he became a trick roper and traveled with a circus. He got his lucky break while appearing in the Ziegfield Follies. Unfortunately, his life was cut short as the result of a plane crash in Alaska. While his most widely-known quote is "I never met a man I didn't like," he is also credited with "Everything is changing. People are taking their comedians seriously and the politicians as a joke."

- The meal Will Rogers enjoyed more than any other was chili con carne, which he dubbed "the bowl of blessedness."

- The dwarf who could spin straw into gold was Rumpelstiltskin.

- Television's Roseanne reportedly earned $40 million in 1995.

- Wilma Rudolph was an Olympic track and field athlete who

won three gold medals at age 20, setting two new world records. She was unable to walk until age 11, because of childhood illnesses of scarlet fever and polio. Five years later, she entered her first Olympics.

- Rock Hudson received his stage name from the Rock of Gibraltar and the Hudson River.

## "R" Places

- Surprisingly, check your map and you'll see that Reno, Nevada, is farther west than Los Angeles.
- Nicknamed "The Rock," Alcatraz Federal Prison was built on an island of 12 acres of solid rock in San Francisco Bay. Some of the most dangerous criminals in the U.S. called Alcatraz home from 1934 until 1963, when it was closed because of the cost of maintaining it. The word Alcatraz has nothing to do with the word rock. It is Spanish for "pelican."
- The city of Rome covers 582 square miles. Although Vatican City lies within Rome, it is an independent country, the smallest one in the world at 1/6 square mile. Its libraries contain about three million books.
- Most of the border between the U.S. and Mexico is formed by the Rio Grande, which translates "Big River." It flows for 1,885 miles.
- If you pass through towns named Woonsocket, Galilee, Jerusalem, Weekapaug, and Quonochontaug, you're in Rhode Island.
- The nickname of Reading, Pennsylvania, is Pretzel City.
- Winter is cold in Reykjavik, Iceland, but not as cold as it is in Chicago, Illinois. Reykjavik's average winter temperature is warmer.

## "R" Cartoon Quiz

- Who is Bullwinkle's "squirrel-y" sidekick? – Rocky
- What's the name of the Jetsons' robot maid? – Rosey
- What is the last name of the Flintstones' best friends Barney, Betty, and Bam-Bam? – Rubble
- Identify Dennis the Menace's dog. – Ruff

# MYSTERIOUS CREATURES
By Mona McKown

## Fact or Fiction?

- Definition: Creature; 1. A being of anomalous, unspecified, or uncertain aspect or nature.

### An Inland Water Monster

- An elusive creature dwells in the 100-mile-long Lake Champlain, which links Vermont and New York State with Canada.  On August 30, 1878, six people on a small yacht saw an extraordinary living thing in the water.  One of the six observed, "two large folds just back of the head projecting above the water, and at some distance, say 50 feet or more behind, two or more folds at what was apparently the tail."  This creature, or perhaps a relative, has been consistently reported over the years.

### Legendary Creatures of Yore

- Medieval Europe was the area of the world where fire-breathing dragons were supposed to have roamed.  These beasts usually had horrible fangs, piercing horns, and pestilential breath.  It was common for them to hold a town hostage, devouring many young virgins until some virtuous knight, armed with a magical sword, would slay the beast.  Even after death the dragon was said to have magical powers.  One drop of its blood could kill instantly, and its teeth, when planted in the earth, would spring up overnight as armed men.

- In the jungles of India was a beast with the body of a lion, the face of a man and the stinging tail of a scorpion. It was known as a Manticore. Not only did it have razor-sharp teeth that could shred anything to ribbons, but its tail could fire lethal stingers as far as 100 feet.

- The Kraken was a Scandinavian sea monster that could grab and sting even the largest ships with its tentacles. The characteristics of this monster reveal it to be a monster-size version of the real-life squid.

- The Basilisk, or the Cockatrice, was a very deadly monster who was said to be part serpent and part rooster. It came from an egg laid by a seven-year-old cock; it was sometimes hatched by a toad who sat on it for nine years. The Basilisk's breath could scorch the earth and its glance was deadly – even to itself.

- The ancient Greeks probably got inspiration for the Hydra from the octopus. The octopus' ability to regenerate lost tentacles is similar to the Hydra's ability to grow more heads if one of the nine is cut off. The great Hercules was sent to kill the serpent, as the second of his 12 labors, and succeeded by burning off the eight mortal heads and burying the ninth, immortal, head under a huge rock.

## Loch Ness Monster

- In Loch Ness, which is a northern lake in Scotland and is 750 feet deep, 24 miles long and varies from 1 to 3 miles wide, some people believe a large animal lives. They have nicknamed her "Nessie." Nessie supposedly has flippers, one or two humps, and a long slender neck.

- Descriptions of the strange creature date back to A.D. 565.

- During the 1930's, reported sightings increased when a new highway was constructed along the lake.

- Eyewitnesses have included a member of Parliament, a World War II commander of a women's auxiliary army-corp unit in Britain, a Nobel Prize-winning chemist, Dr. Richard Synge, and a member of the Royal Observer Corp.

- "The Loch Ness Monster is worthy of consideration if only

because it presents a striking example of mass hallucination...We should find no difficulty in understanding how the animal, once being said to have been seen by a few people, should have shortly after revealed itself to many more." – 1933 E.G. Boulenge, director of the aquarium at the London Zoo.

- In modern times, the story of the Loch Ness Monster begins in 1933. On April 13, 1933, Mr. and Mrs. John MacKay sighted an "enormous animal rolling and plunging" in the loch.

- By October of 1933, there had been twenty sightings and the news of the monster in Loch Ness had spread throughout Great Britain.

- Duke Wetherell, a big-game hunter, had found two fresh footprints of "a very powerful soft-footed animal about twenty feet long." Plaster casts were sent to the Museum of Natural History for verification. Within two weeks the museum reported that the footprints had come from a hippo-leg umbrella stand which had been pressed into the mud.

- In 1934, a photo of Nessie was taken by Dr. Robert Wilson, a London gynecologist. Here finally was proof of Nessie's existence. The photo is dark and grainy, but still eerily shows the monster's head, long neck and one hump. This photograph has become known as the Surgeon's Photograph

and is probably the most popular photo of the creature. However in 1993, some sixty years later, it was discovered the famous photo was also a hoax, concocted by none other than Duke Wetherell, as a means of getting revenge for his previous embarrassment. The Nessie in the photo was made from a toy submarine with a plastic wood head and neck built over the sub's conning tower.

- In 1951 Lachlan Stuart, a forestry worker who lived beside the loch, took a picture of the creature. He noticed a disturbance on the water after which three humps appeared, moving in a line toward the shore.
- The first moving pictures of Nessie came along in 1960. Tim Dinsdale, an aviation engineer, was the cameraman.
- The Loch Ness Phenomena Investigation Bureau was formed in 1961. The Bureau collated, checked, and published all reports of sightings.
- Equipment used to help find the elusive beast included a noise-making machine from the Royal Navy, foul-smelling bait which weighed 50 pounds and was made of dried animal blood, snake hormone and other gruesome ingredients, a one-man American submarine, the Viperfish, and a submersible called the Pisces.

## Mokele-mbembe

- Across central Africa tales of a claw-footed, hippopotamus-sized creature with a long neck and tail have been told for more than two hundred years. This fearsome tropical monster is known to the Congolese people as Mokele-mbembe. In 1980 and 1981 two expeditions were led by Roy P. Mackal, an American biochemist, into the Likouala swamp region in the People's Republic of the Congo. After collecting many first-hand descriptions of the Mokele-mbembe from the Congo natives, it was concluded that there were striking similarities between this creatures size, eating habits and general appearance and those of a small sauropod dinosaur which was thought to have been extinct for more than 60 million years. The formidable conditions of the African Congo have remained unchanged for millions of years, which suggests to some cryptozoologists that it would be possible for dinosaur-like animals to have survived and lived until present day.

## Creaturely Quotes

- "Whoever fights monsters should see to it that in the process he does not become a monster. When you look long into the abyss, the abyss also looks into you." –Friedrich Wilhelm Nietzsch

- "A wonderful fact to reflect upon, that every human creature is constituted to be that profound secret and mystery to every other." – Charles Dickens

- "Noble be man, helpful and good! For that alone sets him apart from every other creature on earth."
  – Johann von Goethe

- "We have found that where science has progressed the farthest, the mind has but regained from nature that which the mind put into nature. We have found a strange footprint on the shores of the unknown. We have devised profound theories, one after another, to account for its origin. At least we have succeeded in reconstructing the creature that made the footprint. And lo! it is our own." – Sir Arthur Eddington

- "Like following life through creatures you dissect, you lose it in the moment you detect." – Alexander Pope

## Yeti or The Abominable Snowman

- In April of 1941, seven men escaped from a Siberian prison camp. They travelled by night and hid by day, avoiding the populated areas. The leader of the escapees was Slavomis Rawicz, who was a member of the Polish army. In almost 2 months the group was 1,200 miles from their prison camp, number 303 in Siberia. They crossed outer Mongolia and Gobi Desert and reached the Himalayas in October of 1941. The friendly Tibetans helped with provisions, sending them on their way across the mountains into India. Reaching the crest of the last mountain range, the men could see there was only one acceptable path of descent, but in the distance they could see two creatures in the path. As the men drew closer to the pair, they saw creatures who were 8 feet tall, rusty brown in color and somewhere between a bear and an ape in appearance. Rawicz later described this encounter between the pair of beasts and the group of men in his book, *The Long Walk*. "Two points struck me immediately. They were enormous and they walked on their hind legs. The picture is clear in my mind, fixed there indelibly by a solid two hours of observation. We just could not believe what we saw at first, so we stayed to watch...I got the uncomfortable feeling they were challenging us to continue our descent across their ground. 'I think, they are laughing at us,' said Zaro. Mister Smith stood up – 'It occurs to me they might take it into their heads to come up and investigate us. It is obvious they are not afraid of us. I think we had better go while we are safe.' We pushed off around the rock and directly away from them. I looked back and the pair were standing still, arms swinging slightly, as though listening intently. What were they? For years they remained a mystery to me but recently I have read of scientific expeditions to discover the Abominable Snowman of the Himalayas and studied descriptions of the creature given by native hill men. I believe that on that day we may have encountered two of the animals." Forced to make a dangerous detour, tragedy struck the little group. One of the men slipped off a rope and fell into a seemingly bottomless crevasse – an indirect victim of the "Abominable Snowman."

## Sasquatch or Bigfoot

- On the Canadian mainland opposite Vancouver Island in 1924 a Scandinavian lumberjack named Albert Ostman went on a combination vacation-prospecting trip at the head of the Tola Inlet on the Powell River. He had hired an old Indian to take him up the river and was told of the giant Sasquatch who supposedly lived in the area. Sasquatch means "wild men of the woods." They are creatures who are hairy but seem human and resemble the Yeti of the Himalayas.

- Ostman took enough food for 3 weeks, a rifle, a sleeping bag, and other basic equipment. When he was well started on his way, he dismissed his Indian guide. He located a good place to spend his first night, hung his supplies on a pole high above the ground and made a bed out of branches. In the morning after he woke he found his things had been disturbed. He thought that a porcupine might have been the cause. The same thing happened on the second night, and Ostman realized that it could not have been a porcupine. The salt which is what porcupines always touch first had not been touched. On the third night he intended to stay awake to see what was coming into his camp. He did not undress, but took off his boots and put them in the bottom of his sleeping bag. Half asleep, he suddenly felt himself being picked up. Still in his sleeping bag, he was thrown over something and carried along. In the confines of his sleeping bag he was carried possibly 30 miles and then dropped to the ground. In the dark he heard voices but could not understand what they were saying. Working his way out of his bag, he looked up and saw four giant creatures, standing on two legs like humans.

- Ostman was being held captive by a Sasquatch family – a mother and father and two children. The father called the "old man" by Ostman, was between 7 feet and 8 feet tall, and was apparently the one who carried him through the woods.

- At daylight, Ostman was able to see he was trapped in a natural bowl high in the mountains with only one way out. He bided his time while he checked his supplies, which had been brought along. There were a few things missing. His snuff was one thing that remained, and it proved to be very useful in his escape.

- Ostman was held captive for seven days. The young male offered him sweet roots and grass to eat. The "old man" and one of the "children" developed a liking for the snuff.

On the seventh day, Ostman offered the snuff to the "old man," who ate what was left. The old man ingested so much of the snuff, he began rolling his eyes and charged off to the spring for water. Ostman made his escape.

- After making his way back to civilization he did not tell his story for many years because he thought no one would believe him. When he finally did tell his story, he gave detailed descriptions of the Sasquatch family who kidnapped him.
- In Willow Creek, California, there is a huge redwood statue of a Bigfoot in the middle of town. Each year the townspeople hold a carnival called "Bigfoot Daze." There are footprints in the sidewalks, like Grauman's Chinese Theater, and Bigfoot ashtrays and rings are for sale in all the gift shops.
- Bigfoot sightings have been made all over the United States and Canada, in 49 states and 4 Canadian provinces.
- In 1892, in Anaconda, Montana, an individual reported seeing a hairy 'varmit' in the mountains.
- Near Seeley Lake, Montana, in 1959 a bear hunter saw Bigfoot but did not shoot it.
- In November of 1962, Reed Christenson, his wife and daughter reported seeing a 6 to 7 foot Bigfoot run up an embankment beside a road at Lost Trail Pass in Montana.

## Giant Squid

- Until the 1870's the giant squid was considered a mythical sea monster. It was in the 1870's that a dozen or so giant squid were reported in Newfoundland. Most were found stranded on the shores and a few were examined and identified by experts.
- On October 26, 1873, Daniel Squires, Thiophilus Piccot, and his twelve-year-old son Tom were setting out to net herring off the southeastern tip of Newfoundland. They had settled in their small flat-bottomed boat, which was about twenty feet long, and had rowed a short way out into Conception Bay. They soon noticed what appeared to be a raft of seaweed, but as their boat drew nearer, they realized it was not. The

thing's surface was slick and purplish red. One of the men poked the strange mound with a boat hook and suddenly the creature erupted, forming eight long, thick, sucker-studded arms in a circle. At the center of these eight arms was a long parrot-like beak and a pair of eyes, the size of dinner plates. A pair of tentacles, twice as long as the squid's arms, darted towards the small boat. Within seconds the giant squid had wrapped its tentacle around the boat and was pulling it and its occupants toward its open mouth. The fishermen were frantically hitting the giant creature with their oars. Tom picked up a hatchet and managed to chop off the arm and tentacle that were holding the small boat. It was then that the monster retreated into a great cloud of inky fluid. Quickly, the men rowed to shore with the tentacle and arm still attached to the boat, as evidence of their encounter. The tentacle stretched nineteen feet and was only a portion of its total length.

## The Last Look

- In rural England on February 8, 1855, a group of surprised villagers discovered countless numbers of unidentifiable tracks in the snow. The tracks were seen in 18 communities in the county of Devon. The tracks were shaped like horseshoes but ran in absolutely straight lines – one directly behind another. In a single night the unknown creature travelled about 100 miles. In some places the thing had apparently walked right up walls and along the rooftops. Here and there the tracks gave the impression that the creature had actually gone through walls and roofs. For some time the people of Devon County were afraid to go out after dark.

# MISCELLANEOUS FACTS
By V. B. Darrington

- Edith Hechter of Brisbane, Australia, was charged with mayhem against her own husband. The hot-headed housewife gouged out her husband's eye when he commented that her new hairdo made her face look fat!
- Of course you may already know that St. Andrew is the patron saint of travelers. But did you know that St. George is the saint of Boy Scouts, and St. Apollonia is the saint of dentists? There are patron saints for nearly every profession, including pawnbrokers, gravediggers, secretaries, and even clowns!
- At a university graduation ceremony in Sefrou, Morocco, guests and graduates were shocked when approximately 50 vultures started dive-bombing the crowd. People scattered in pandemonium as the huge birds swooped just above their heads. No one has quite figured out what caused the vultures to attack so brazenly, but college officials aren't taking any chance —next year's graduation ceremony will be held indoors.
- The convenience of your cellular phone comes with a risk. Researchers found that car phone users run a 34 percent higher risk of having an accident. Usually, motorists caught up in phone conversations run red lights and get into collisions at busy intersections. But chatty drivers can even be dangerous on the open road. "They kind of forget about the rest of the world," says John Violanti, a criminal justice professor.
- What weighs 100 tons, is 1,500 years old and spans 37 acres?

Believe it or not, it's a mushroom! The "Armillorie bulbosa, as it's known by scientists who discovered it in the woods near Crystal Falls, Michigan, is the largest living organism on the planet. The giant fungus has

been growing in the forest for almost 2,000 years, according to Dr. J.N. Bruhn of Michigan Technological University. "In all my years of research I have never seen anything this incredible and probably never will again," Dr. Bruhn said.

- Are you an only child? Contrary to popular belief, the only child is no smarter or more spoiled than children who have brothers and sisters. That's the finding of three Bowling Green State University (Ohio) sociologists who studied 7,512 adults, including 845 only children. The researchers discovered that the "onlies" did have slightly more education, but that's because their parents were able to spend more money on them.

- Timothy McGregor, 42, of Brisbane, Australia survived a plane wreck, two auto accidents, a lightning strike, and deadly cancer—only to die from an infected mosquito bite! Known as "Mr. Lucky," the man had become famous for his ability to escape death and was a minor celebrity in his hometown. Authorities say he was bitten by a mosquito on a camping trip and had contracted a fatal infection by the time he saw a doctor.

- A taxi driver in Cancun, Mexico, had a day to remember. Early in his shift he was called upon to aid a woman as she delivered a baby boy in his cab on route to the hospital. The excitement of the moment soon was eclipsed by another opportunity for heroism in the afternoon. Jose Arias noticed that his passenger was acting odd, and turning blue. He screeched to a stop and saved the man from choking by performing the Heimlich maneuver. But the day wasn't over—

in the evening, Jose witnessed some hoods as they mugged an elderly couple. Jose chased them down in his cab and radioed for police. Jose received a special commendation for his heroics of a single day!

## That's Life

- In a gruesome case of extreme irony, the son of the inventor of Lifesavers candy drowned himself by throwing himself overboard from a ship in 1933.

- Lovestruck Gina Farretti's family forbade her to marry her longtime boyfriend—-so 78-year-old Gina and her 91-year-old beau eloped!

- A lot of dentists put fish tanks in their lobbies because they believe they calm their patients' nerves—but the idea has backfired! A two-year study shows an increasing

number of Americans don't like seeing fish tanks because they remind them of going to the dentist.

- Don't let your druggist make a mistake on a prescription—it could be hazardous to your health. A study in <u>Annals Of Pharmacotherapy</u> revealed that out of 30,000 prescriptions examined over a nine-month period, 623 contained mistakes. But don't get paranoid. Surveys have consistently revealed that pharmacists are the most trusted professionals in America.

- Doctors' hand-writing is notoriously terrible. But don't blame the doctor if you can't read your prescription. It is written in abbreviated Latin. Use the list below to crack your doctor's code on your next prescription: "Rx"-take (from the Latin for recipe), "ac"-before meals (ante cibum),"pc"-after meals (post cibum), "qh"-every hour (quague hora), "bid"-twice per day (dis in die), "tid"-three per day (ter in die), "qid"-four per day (quater in die), "hs"-at bedtime (hora somni), "po"-by mouth (per os), "prn"-as needed (pro re nata).

- Hollywood is the land of the smooth walkers. But Tinsel Town has yet to replace the legendary walk of Marilyn Monroe. Few realized that Marilyn's famous wiggle was caused by the fact that the heel of one of her shoes was custom-built shorter than the other by half an inch!

- It's a good bet you don't know that there is one slot machine for every eight inhabitants in Las Vegas. Residents of the great state of Nevada bet an average of $846 a year in gambling casinos.

- Famed train robber Jesse James was also a publisher! While in prison with the Younger brothers in Minnesota in 1887, the gunslinging outlaw contributed $50 to start a prison newspaper. The paper, "The Prison Mirror," still publishes—and has won many coveted journalism awards!

- Each week, America's cows belch up an incredible 184,569 tons of methane gas—enough to boil 800 million gallons of water!

- The tallest, professional actors on record are James (Marshal Dillon) Arness, Bruce Spence and Christopher (Dracula) Lee. Gunsmoke's Arness measured up at 6 feet 7 inches, along with Spence, who starred in "The Stork" (Australia 1971). Horror actor Lee comes in at a respectable 6 feet 5 inches.

- About 1,150 Americans in l00,000 are likely to reach their 100th birthday, according to analysis of recent statistics. Women have a much better chance of reaching that age than men: 1,927 women versus 423 men per 100,000. Around 1900, just 31 people in 100,000 reached that milestone in life.

- Raising a child born in 1990 to age 18, not including any college, will cost more than $1 million, according to a newly released study. The report stated that the US government's estimate of $65,250 failed to take into account inflation and other miscellaneous items, and did not include the lost income of a parent staying at home to raise the child.

- A brand-new survey of American pet owners finds that the rat, far from being the despised rodent that many people believe it to be, is the fourth most popular pet in the country! According to the survey, these are our top six pets, in order of popularity: 1. Dogs; 2. Cats; 3. Birds (parakeets and canaries); 4. Rats (white and brown rats); 5. Fish; and 6. Ocelots.

- It was a dream come true for all the failing students at Valparaiso High School in Indiana, when a computer mix-up switched the grades on the report cards. "The scanner read high grades as low and low grades as high," says superintendent Michael Benway. Some kids were really surprised and didn't want to give their cards back!"

## More Miscellany

- In perhaps one of the stinkiest ways people have tried to beat the immigration system, California border police discovered 17 Mexicans crammed into a porta potty. The tiny toilet was strapped into the back of pickup truck driven by three US citizens, who were held on charges of smuggling illegal aliens. The porta john was a larger model that allows for handicap access, but the quarters were still unbelievably cramped. "They were pretty much stacked up inside there", says spokesman Ron Henley. "It was quite a feat getting them all inside."

- Doctors in Shanghai removed 1,650 gallstones from a woman's gallbladder which had swollen to the size of a pear. Zhu Ping, 47, suffered from gallstones for more than 10 years, despite numerous treatments by Chinese and Western medicine. The surgeons say such a number of gallstones in a patient is unheard of. Zhu Ping returned home a day after the operation.

- What's going to be the next hot new diet food? Try Jellyfish! Believe it or not, nutritionists claim jellyfish are the perfect high-protein fat free food. And they're already an ultra-popular delicacy in China and Taiwan, where top chefs remove the tentacles and serve the bulb-like body with sweet or spicy seasoning

- A study done in Nice, France, shows you can improve your mood—simply by changing the color of the clothes you wear! Psychologists at Nice University have proven that wearing bright colors like red, orange and yellow can enhance a person's perception of his or her environment and brighten his or her spirits.

- A cemetery outside Sydney, Australia, is located on the corner of Lost Avenue and Soul Street.

- Why is there supposed to be seven years' bad luck when you break a mirror? In ancient times it was assumed that one's image in the glass was a reflection of a person's soul. And the Romans believed the soul was renewed every seven years. Hence, you'll have seven year's bad luck - until your inner self renews itself.

## Things You Need To Know

- Morris Odell Mason wasn't worried about cholesterol when he ordered four Big Macs, two large fries, two hot fudge sundaes, and a hot apple pie from his prison cell in Virginia in 1985. It was his last meal!

- Here's a look at what some other condemned prisoners have ordered as they prepared to face their executioners: Leon Moser, Pennsylvania, 1995-cheese pizza, cheese slices, cold cuts, pasta salad, iced cupcakes, and a Coke; Richard Beavers, Texas, 1994-French toast, barbecued spare ribs, scrambled eggs and bacon, sausage patties, french fries, three slices of cheese, two pieces of cake, and four cartons of milk; James Smith, Texas, 1990-yogurt; Ted Bundy, Florida, 1989-steak, hash browns, and coffee; Gary Gilmore, Utah, 1977-hamburger, eggs, and coffee.

- If you are a parent too impatient to wait for the V-chip to block out unwanted television shows, then try the TV Terminator. The Terminator is a universal remote control shaped like a pistol and offered by TVT Inc. The $49.95 item lets couch potato cops take aim at the screen and zap channels along with sound effects like "boos" and gunfire. "Men like to relive their childhood fantasies by shooting the bad guys," says Sheldon Silverman of TVT.

- To err is human—and it's good for you. Psychologists have found that mistakes are actually " powerful and unique learning opportunities." Society researchers looked into mistakes made by 230 prominent people and concluded the fear of "making" a mistake causes more damage than the actual mistakes.

- If you pick the morning for projects that challenge the mind, you're making a big mistake. Researchers of England's Cambridge University have discovered that your brain functions more efficiently in the afternoon. "Contrary to what people often think—that we are fresh, enthusiastic and efficient at our work first thing in the morning—our evidence shows that we are better at intellectual work later in the day.", declared research psychologist Dr. Keith Millar. It isn't that we make more mistakes. It's just that we are slower in the morning. Although our mental performance increases as the day goes on, we do have a sluggish period for a few hours after lunch. It seems that our body clock slows down in the early afternoon in an attempt to urge our bodies to relax and go to sleep. Dr. Millar recommends that we listen to our body by taking an afternoon nap, and then working later into the evening. Dr. Millar's study indicates that we should tackle repetitive tasks that don't involve much brainwork  in the morning, while our intellectual tasks should be reserved for later in the day.

# 24

# WEDDINGS
by J. C. Walker

### Wedded Blitz

- Most of the customs we associate with wedding ceremonies are derived from old English and European practices that made sense to brides and grooms in ancient times. The word "<u>wedding</u>" originally meant "promise" or "pledge." Many traditions – wearing a veil, carrying the bride over the threshold, and throwing rice – were observances meant to ward off evil spirits during the happy event. The "honeymoon" literally comes from the French word <u>lune de miel</u>, or "moon of honey" – in the Middle Ages a couple would drink from a potion containing honey on each of the first 30 days of their marriage.

- Getting hitched is a universal human experience, even though the details of marriage ceremonies vary all over the world. In Eastern Orthodox weddings, the couple wear special crowns of precious metals or even lemon branches during the ceremony. In India they wear long flower leis and consult their astrological charts at the beginning of the event. Muslim marriages for the rich can last up to three full days at the bride's home. In Japan, marriage vows are finalized as both bride and groom take three sips of sake at the conclusion of the ceremony.

### No Mickey Mouse Weddings

- Here in the U.S., weddings are high-ticket items, and even Mickey Mouse has gotten into the wedding business. At

Disney World in Florida, the big cheese has thoughtfully provided a special Wedding Pavilion for happy couples who really do want to start life together in Fantasyland, and the price tag runs anywhere from $2,500 for just the bride and groom to over $20,000 for a 100-guest event. This grand package includes the usual wedding observances with unique Magic Kingdom touches – a ceremony in front of Cinderella's castle, royal trumpeters, a theme banquet, Cinderella's horse-drawn coach, rings presented in a glass slipper, and Tinkerbell in attendance. More realistic couples, who see marriage as the adventure it really is, can opt instead to tie the knot in the 13-story free-fall Tower of Terror ride.

## Get It In Writing

- Throughout history, though, people have usually been a lot more realistic than to expect the likes of Tinkerbell to show up at their weddings. Scientists have discovered ancient Egyptian documents, clearly pre-nuptial agreements, which were used to wrap sacred mummified crocodiles. Some of the documents date as far back as 300 B.C.

## And A New Groom?

- A woman in Tallahassee, Florida, is suing a beauty salon for ruining her wedding. Seems she went to the hairdressers about a month before her wedding in 1994 to have her hair frosted, and the coloring was left on just a little too long. Her hair turned yellow, and subsequent efforts turned it black and then orange. Sores developed on her scalp. In desperation, she asked the salon to have extensions woven into her hair to make it look more

normal. She said it made her "look like Cousin Itt." She's suing for $15,000 to cover the cost of another wedding and reception – a wedding re-do as it were. "Another honeymoon and a new ceremoney for me to feel normal again," she said.

## An Offer You Can't Refuse

- A great Italian bridal tradition could bear reviving – the dowry cookbook. Not only did Italian grooms receive the usual goats, land, and olive oil when they married, they also received access to the bride's cherished family recipes. These recipes were jealously guarded as they were passed down from mother to daughter, and that was often the only way the groom's family could gain access to them.

## American Gladiators

- One of the great traditions for brides in the Boston area is the annual Filene's Department Store wedding gown sale. For over fifty years, on one special day every fall, brides have pressed against the locked doors of the store in anticipation of saving hundreds or even thousands of dollars on designer and high-end gowns. When the doors finally open at 8 a.m., the more aggressive types run through the store grabbing any dress in any size they can manage. This gives them the option of choosing later which one they want so they can benevolently pass off the discards to the more timid shoppers. Store management wisely mixes sizes on the racks so individuals can't completely monopolize fittings, and women unabashedly shed street clothing to try on gowns right in the store aisles. Friends will "stand guard" over special finds, as shoppers usually pay $249 for dresses that cost as much as $2,000. Filene spokespeople say the sale lasts about a minute. That's how long it usually takes for the racks to be stripped bare.

## Not a Filene's Bride

- Two of Mexico's most popular singers well known for their romantic ballads, Lucero Hogaza and Manuel Mijares, recently married in a huge Mexico City wedding that was broadcast live all over Central and South America. It was attended by 300 of their closest friends in the old San Ignacio Loyola chapel, officiated by Archbishop Norberto Rivera Carrera, and the vows blessed by Pope John Paul. The bride wore a glittering gown with a 15-foot train. Music was provided by an orchestra, and outside 200 police patrolled the area to prevent gate-crashers from inviting themselves into the nuptials. At the reception, 1,500 more friends joined the wedding party and danced 'til dawn. The bride and groom then departed on a 45-day honeymoon cruise to Japan and the Far East.While the happy couple are not making public statements about their wedding day, insiders estimate the get-together cost upwards of 14 million dollars.

## Kid Stuff

- For those of you who believe in long engagements, you'll be happy to hear about the couple in Shasta, California, who recently tied the knot in their old kindergarten classroom – that's how long they had known each other. Even though they had gone to school together, Jennifer Beck and Toby Miller had never dated until after her first marriage ended, but, the bride said, they were set up on a blind date when "Toby just kept popping into my mind."

## Double-Ring Indemnity

- People spend a lot on weddings these days, so they're not just events, they're investments. That's why a growing trend in high-end nuptials is wedding insurance. The policies – the base price is $129 – will cover almost every disaster that can befall that special day. Military call-ups, natural disasters, death or illness of someone in the wedding party, damaged film negatives, ruined wedding attire and stolen gifts are just a few of the nightmares that can be rectified with wedding insurance. It will even cover the cost of human error, too – if the photographer forgets to load the camera with film, the insurance will pay to recreate the wedding completely, right down to flying your bridesmaids back to town and buying a new wedding cake. There's only one thing the insurance company won't cover, however. "If you change your mind, sorry, because we just can't track the course of Cupid's arrow with any accuracy," they said.

## No Thanks for the Memories

- A chocolate Labrador retriever attended his owner's wedding as a flower girl, dressed in a red collar, white ribbons and a wreath. The four-legged attendant performed his duties perfectly but was not permitted in the clubhouse for the reception. There are also unverified reports that increasing numbers of family dogs are serving as ring bearers in their owners' ceremonies.

- One couple in Florida planned a formal poolside wedding and showed up looking a little underdressed – the bride wore a white bikini, while the groom's outfitted himself in white shorts and matching bow tie.

- Another Florida couple were married standing in their swamp buggy. He had proposed to her during an Everglade party in the vehicle, and she thought that would be a romantic way to say their vows. The ceremony was solemnized when the bride's brother dunked her in the swamp mud.

- "When two people are under the influence of the most violent, most insane, most delusive, and most transient of passions, they are required to swear that they will remain in that excited, abnormal and exhausting condition until death do them part."

– George Bernard Shaw

## Not Even Near-Beer

- While we're on the subject of unusual weddings, a recent wedding in the Ukraine was so different it made the international news. Apparently the women of the village Lviv had had enough of their husbands' affinity for frequent nips of vodka, and alcohol was banned at public celebrations and on holidays. New Year's Eve this year was alcohol-free for the first time. According to the new village edicts, husbands who arrive at work obviously inebriated spend their days raking dung in a local pigsty. This has not been a hit with

Lviv menfolk who are quite irate about their spouses' new-found determination. Resistence evaporated after one overindulged citizen who passed out in public woke to find his head had been shaved. The village womens' final <u>coup de grace</u> was a wedding which was, for the first time in the town's history, celebrated without drunkenness.

## Dovetailed

- One Rhode Island couple has found a whole new way to keep that wedding day joy coming. They own a company named Love Birds, Inc., and their job is to provide doves to perform at weddings all along the Eastern seaboard. Two doves are specially trained to alight simultaneously from the bride and groom's hands after the ceremony, while 40 "chorus line" doves flutter and rise to the sky behind them in a breathtaking moment of choreographed nuptial splendor. While the birds may show up at the wedding in picturesque wicker baskets, they pay their own fare home and show up at their owners' back porch a few hours later.

## And the Color Is Perfect

- A young Norwegian couple got a wedding gift that will keep on giving. While traveling during their engagement in Belarus (part of the former Soviet Union) last year, they learned of a congregation in the town of Berezino that was so poor it could not afford a church. David Holme and Ingunn Lyngset decided the best wedding present they could have would be to give the people who had shown them much kindness a church. When they sent invitations to their wedding last year, they included requests for cash donations rather than gifts. Although a few guests resisted, all eventually agreed and presented the bride and groom with $17,200 in cash, which has since been used to buy a building in Berezino and renovate it. Earlier this year, they returned with the second half of their wedding present, a load of construction materials to complete the overhaul of the building. The couple has no regrets about their decision: "We had to follow our hearts," Ingunn said.

## And Baby Makes Three

- Still, the most newsworthy wedding last year was that of Susu and Mike, in Lopburi, Thailand. Dressed in golden clothes and jasmine flower garlands, they were married on TV, and recently announced the birth of a child. The happy couple are orangutans.

## Ain't Got Those Wedding Bell Blues

- Wedding planner Fay Baldwin of Madisonville, Kentucky, has her own collection of wedding stories just too different to forget. While the most elaborate she's ever presented was a high-class Hindu nuptial, many others would take the wedding cake for being unique. She recalls the couple who won a wedding at the Wave Pool at Holiday World in Santa Claus, Indiana ("It was hard keeping it from looking like a baptism"), many Western weddings decorated with straw and saddles, twelve couples who married en masse on a rollercoaster, and numerous wedding vows taken on the local waterslide. A few she probably did against her better judgement But she's learned to keep her opinions to herself, with good reason – she's already had five brides hire her to plan each of their three weddings. While most of Baldwin's clients spend an average of $2,000 for her services, some have spent as much as $40,000.

# WINTER SPORTS
By Kathy Wolfe

## First Fact

- 25 countries on three continents must participate in a sport before it is considered for the Winter Olympics.

## Hockey Bits

- Scandinavians most likely invented the sport of skating by strapping ox or elk bones to their boots. In fact, the word <u>skate</u> originates from "schake," which means "leg bone."
- The game of hockey originated in Canada, with the first game supposedly played in 1855 in Ontario.
- Although the NHL wasn't formed until 1917, Stanley Cup Playoffs began in 1894. The first playoff game was in Montreal before 5,000 fans.
- In 1908, the top salary for a hockey player was $1,800 a season.
- The first artificial ice rinks came along in the 1890's in New York and Baltimore.
- The Toronto hockey team started out as the Toronto Arenas. They were later known as the St. Patricks, and finally became the Maple Leafs in 1927.
- The New York Rangers, the Chicago Black Hawks, and the Detroit Red Wings have all been in existence since 1926.
- Early hockey team names included the Blueshirts, the Millionaires, the Silver Seven, the Wanderers, the Shamrocks, and the Thistles.
- Mervin Dutton was wounded in World War I by 48 fragments

of shrapnel from an exploding shell. When doctors told him his leg would have to be amputated, he refused, citing his love of hockey. His leg was placed at a 30½ angle for 14 months; Dutton recovered, going on to play professional hockey and to serve as President of the NHL.

- The blade of a hockey skate is about 12" long, but the blade of a speed skate can be up to 18".

- At the first seven Olympic winter games, Canada took the gold medal in hockey six times. In 1956, the Soviets took over, and took 7 out of the next 9 Olympic gold medals, with their only losses in 1960 and 1980. Quite a feat considering that ice hockey had never been played in Russia before World War II.

- The Russian Olympic losses of 1960 and 1980 were made possible by the U.S. team. Who doesn't remember the 1980 Olympic hockey team who defeated the most powerful team in the world? Only one week before, the Soviets had hammered the U.S. 10-3 in an exhibition game. The heart-rending Olympic game had a final score of 4-3, and was so moving, it became known as the "Miracle on Ice." This, however, was not the game that won the U.S. the gold medal — they went on to defeat Finland in the gold medal round.

- The coach for the "Miracle on Ice" team of 1980 was Herb Brooks. Herb had been an Olympic hockey player, too; in fact, he was the last player to be cut from the American team in 1960. That year was the only other time the U.S. won a gold medal in hockey–but without Herb.

- It's a family affair — Bill Christian and his brother Roger played on the winning 1960 Olympic hockey team. Bill's son David was a player on the 1980 "Miracle on Ice" team.

- The Olympic hockey rink is about 15 feet wider than the NHL rink.

- Bobby Orr was playing organized hockey at age , and attracted the attention of NHL scouts when he was 12. He began playing Junior A hockey at 14, playing against young men five years older.

- Gordie Howe spent 26 seasons with the Detroit Red Wings, retiring in 1971. He holds the record for the most seasons played and the most regular-season games – 1,767. He was the NHL MVP six times.
- A <u>Sports Illustrated</u> survey voted Ulf Samuelsson of the New York Rangers as hockey's most annoying player. He was listed as "the most hated man in hockey. Plays dirty and admits it."
- Sergei Fedorov defected to the U.S. from Russia and now plays for the Detroit Red Wings. This 1994 NHL MVP contributes his success to the fact that he "thinks like a puck".
- If you're sitting at a hockey game, and all of a sudden the fans begin throwing their hats on the rink, it's because one player has scored three goals in the same game, aptly named a "hat trick." Wayne Gretzky holds the record for the most hat tricks. It's not a term original to hockey. It was in the sport of cricket that it was first used. A player who bowled three consecutive wickets received a new hat.
- "All pro athletes are bilingual. They speak English and profanity." – Gordie Howe
- Dave Manson of the Winnipeg Jets wins the award for the fastest shot in the NHL. He smacked the puck at a record 98 mph.
- Hockey pucks are frozen before each game to make them harder and faster.
- By the time he was 14, The Great Gretzky already had 1,000 goals in organized hockey to his credit.
- The name Frank Zamboni is a very important one to the sport of hockey. He is the inventor of the 6,480-lb. machine that resurfaces the ice. The machine holds 260 gallons of water and cruises along the ice at 9 mph.

## It Figures

- Sonja Henie of Norway competed in her first Olympics at age 11 in 1924, the year of the first Winter Olympics, where she came in dead last. She was world champion at age 14, and went on to win three gold medals, in 1928, 1932, and 1936. Sonja was a favorite of Adolph Hitler. She performed her programs on outdoor rinks in the cold and wind in a knee-length wool skirt. However, she didn't need to worry about her skirt's hampering her jumps. In her day it was deemed "unladylike to jump into the air" or perform spins. (Today, seven triple jumps is the average for a skating program.) Sonja retired at age 23, moved to Hollywood, and became a millionaire actress.

- Figure skaters perform many triple axels, but what exactly is a triple axel, and where did the name come from? It is a move created by Axel Paulsen, in which the skater launches into the air off one foot, spins around 3 times, and lands on the opposite foot, going backward. Don't confuse this with the Lutz, in which the skater starts out backward, leaps into the air off the toe pick, spins 3 times, and lands on the same foot.

- Eric Heiden, who set five men's speed-skating records at the 1980 Olympics, retired from skating and went on to become a professional bike racer. He is now a doctor in California.

- In 1968, the Winter Olympics were held in Grenoble, France. Peggy Fleming was America's ice princess, but unfortunately fell during her freestyle program. However, her lead was sufficient to earn her the gold medal, the only one taken home by an American that year.

- Nancy Kerrigan advises that after a big spin, when you're very dizzy, don't go for a hard move immediately after. Alleviate the dizziness by bending your knees.

- The U.S. won only one gold medal at the 1964 Winter Olympics — in speed skating. And the winner was wearing skates he'd had to borrow from his coach.

- Short-track speed skating became an official event in 1992. Four skaters race in a pack around a 400-meter track with padded walls.

- A skater from the Netherlands skated a record 339 miles in a 24-hour period in 1988.

# Sleds And Such

- Bobsledding takes place on a track that is actually a chute of ice. In a 60-second run, the fiberglass sled reaches speeds of 90 mph.
- Eddie Egan was the Olympic lightweight boxing champion of 1920. At the 1932 Winter Olympics in Lake Placid, he won in the bobsled category, making him the first person to win in both summer and winter Olympics.
- When it became apparent how important a fast start is to a bobsled run, teams began recruiting the best track and field runners. Willie Davenport won a gold medal in hurdles in the Summer Olympics and went on to the Winter Olympics twelve years later on a bobsled team.
- The movie <u>Cool Runnings</u> was no joke. Jamaica, the tropical island where it never snows, did in fact send a bobsled team to the 1988 Olympics. The team had trained on a concrete slope on a bobsled with wheels. Unfortunately, at the competition in Albertville, France, their sled crashed and the team couldn't finish.
- Robin Todhunter of Great Britain was proud to complete the most famous sled run in the world at St. Moritz, Switzerland, in 1987. Especially because he was nearly 84-years-old when he did it.
- If lying on your back on a sled and shooting down an ice chute feet first at speeds of 75 mph sounds like fun, then perhaps the luge is for you. You'll need a rubberized suit, a crash helmet with a face shield, gloves with metal spikes on the fingers, and a 50-lb. fiberglass sled. The track is three-quarters of a mile long and the run takes about 45 seconds to complete.
- The word <u>luge</u> is French for <u>sled</u>.
- The three women lugers from East Germany had an interesting strategy for winning the 1968 Olympics. They heated the runners of their sleds, causing the ice to melt, speeding up their sleds. Unfortunately, this "strategy" was discovered, and they were all disqualified.

180

- There has never been an American gold medalist in luge, maybe because there wasn't even a track for it until one had to be built for the 1980 Olympics at Lake Placid.
- While the Iditarod is probably the most famous dog-sled race, the 1,049-mile trail from Anchorage to Nome is not the longest. The longest race takes place annually in Markovo, Russia, the 1,243-mile-long Benergia Trail.
- Rev. Donald McEwen drove a team of 76 Siberian and Alaskan huskies for two miles, setting a record for the largest dog-sled team ever.

## Downhill All The Way

- A ski found in Sweden has been carbon-dated back to 3,000 B.C.
- It was Norwegian emigrants who brought the sport of skiing to America in the mid-1800's. At that time, skis were over 9 feet long. The legend of "Snowshoe Thompson" tells about a strapping young Norwegian looking for work during the California gold rush. He took the job of delivering mail across the Sierra Nevada Mountains. He made the 150-mile round trip in five days, with supplies and a 50-lb. mail sack on his back.

- In 1970, Yuichiro Miura of Japan skied 1.6 miles down Mt. Everest, reaching top speed of 93.6 mph.
- Squaw Valley, California, was the site of the 1960 Olympics, and the skiers were more than a little nervous as the competition approached. The reason there was no snow! A local Native American tribe, the Piute, were recruited to do a "snow dance," which miraculously produced the snow needed to save the Games.

- A Finnish Nordic skier traveled 258.2 miles in only 24 hours in April of 1988.
- Only one-hundredth of a second separated the first and the second place winners in the 1980 Olympic cross-country ski race.
- Although it appears that Alpine ski jumpers are miles above the ground, in reality they are only ten feet above the hillside.
- In 1974, Anders Haugen of the United States received his bronze medal for ski jumping. The unusual thing was that Anders was 83-years-old. He had actually competed in 1924, but because of an addition error, was calculated as the fourth-place finisher. It was 50 years later that a researcher discovered the blooper.
- Combine surfing, skiing, and skateboarding and you have the sport of snowboarding. Its popularity began to build in the mid-1980's.

## Final Fact

- Originally, the biathlon was a military training exercise. It combines cross-country skiing and rifle marksmanship over a 12-mile course. The athlete must quickly switch from strenuous skiing with a rifle on his back to the intense focus of shooting. He must shoot ten times standing and ten times lying down.

# I'LL BET YOU DIDN'T KNOW
## by V. B. Darrington

- The Atlantic and Pacific Oceans are more than 2,500 miles apart in most of the United States. But in some places in Central America, the world's two biggest oceans are separated by fewer than 50 miles of land. Panama is the narrowest part of Central America, but there are no mountains in Panama that offer a view of both oceans. However, a peak in the neighboring country of Costa Rica, the 11,325-foot Mount Izaru, is the only point in the world from which you can see both oceans.

- It sounds strange to say that rain keeps the earth dry, but that's exactly what it does. The process that generates precipitation gathers moisture from the air and concentrates it in clouds, which later deposit the water in the form of rains. If this moisture didn't condense to form rain, then the atmosphere would be unbearably humid. The entire earth would be heavily covered with moisture, and life as we know it probably couldn't exist.

## It's Against The Law

- In Gary, Indiana, it's against the law to take a streetcar or go to a theater within four hours after eating garlic.
- In Massachusetts, it's against the law to use tomatoes when making clam chowder.
- In 1659, it was against the law in Massachusetts to celebrate Christmas.
- It's against the law in Seattle, Washington, for goldfish to ride on a bus, unless they lie still.

- It's against the law in California to set a trap for a mouse unless you have a hunting license.

- Books about outlaws are banned in Alabama.
- In Corvallis, Oregon, it's against the law for a young woman to drink coffee after 6 p.m.
- In Atlanta, Georgia, it's illegal for a smelly person to board a streetcar.
- In Pocatello, Idaho, it is a legal offense to look "gloomy."
- In the state of Nebraska, it is illegal for a tavern keeper to sell beer unless he also serves soup at the same establishment.
- In Tennesee, it is against the law to remove the hook from a fish caught by someone else.
- In Houston, Texas, you would be crossing the law if you were to sell goose liver, limburger cheese, or rye bread on Sunday.
- It's against the law to peel an orange in a hotel room if you are in California.
- Animals may be sent to jail in Illinois.
- In Iowa, it is illegal to keep a horse if you live in an apartment building.
- In Connecticut, the law states that merchants cannot sell pickles that will fall apart if dropped from 12 inches.
- Don't try to eat peanuts in church if you are in Massachusetts; it's against the law.
- Little Rock, Arkansas, does not allow dogs to bark after 6 p.m.

- It's illegal in Hartford, Connecticut, to walk across the street on your hands.
- In the United States, the law prohibits the postmaster from hunting ducks.
- In San Francisco, you can be cited for walking an elephant without a leash.

## Fact

- A sign painter was having a hard time fitting the words *motor hotel* onto a sign. So, to save space, he invented the word *motel*.

## Quick Bits

- Did you ever hear of "American Flag" or "Licorice Lulu?" They're the names of flavors of chewing gum that were made and sold over 100 years ago. These gums were made in Maine by two brothers named Curtis. It was packaged under the name of "State of Maine Pure Spruce Gum."
- The Fighting Fish of Siam make their egg nests out of spit and bubbles.
- Christopher Columbus is a famous name in U.S. history. But did you ever hear of Bartholomew Columbus? Chris and Bart were brothers. They planned the ocean voyage together, and both traveled about Europe trying to raise money for the trip. But then Chris got the money he needed and sailed without his brother. No one knows why Bart got left behind. But if he hadn't, Americans might have a holiday called "Columbuses Day."
- A baby sea lion cannot swim from birth. It has to be taught by its mother.
- St. John's Lane, a street in Rome, is only 19 inches wide.
- Ants sometimes get drunk. This happens when ants drink nectar from the bodies of certain beetles. Then "undrunk" ants carry a drunk ant to some water and toss it in. The drunk ant sobers up quickly after his dunking!
- Guinea pigs did not originate in Guinea, nor are they members of the pig family.

- There are full-grown sharks that measure only five inches long.
- People spend about a third of their lives asleep.

## More Quick Bits

- If all the eggs of a female fly hatched, she would be the mother of 131,000,000,000,000,000,000 baby flies in six months.
- Once U.S. President Theodore "Teddy" Roosevelt was on a hunting trip in Mississippi. One day a bear cub was brought into camp for the President to shoot. Roosevelt refused. Because of Teddy Roosevelt's liking for the bear cub, toy bears are called "Teddy bears" to this day.
- America bought Alaska from the Russians for two cents an acre.
- Since serving soda water on Sundays was against the law in the 1800's in most U.S. towns, some drugstore owners could not serve ice cream sodas. Instead they served a concoction with ice cream, nuts, fruit, and syrup but no soda water. These "sundaes" on Sunday became so popular that they were soon served every day of the week.
- Francis Scott Key composed the words to "The Star Spangled Banner" on the back of an envelope.
- You breathe about 3500 gallons of air every day.
- The motto of the famous Pinkerton Detective Agency is "We Never Sleep," and that motto is printed over a picture of an open eye. That's why private detectives are referred to as "Private Eyes."
- Next time you watch an Alfred Hitchcock movie, watch for his famous silhouette. You see, Alfred Hitchcock is "notorious" for always filming a brief scene of himself in each of his movies. His appearances add a moment of humor to his trademark suspense thrillers.
- Other modern-day producers sometimes copy this device. Ron Howard of "Opie" fame frequently films short segments of his various family members.
- The temperature in South Dakota once went from 10 below zero to 55 above zero within the space of two minutes.

- The reason moths and other nocturnal insects circle your porch lamp is not because they crave the spotlight. Moths and insects use the moon to help them navigate in the dark. When an insect gets too close to a light, it does what nature tells it to do-it keeps its body aligned in relation to the light source. If the light source were the far distant moon, the insect would fly straight. However, since the light is so close, the bug ends up flying in circles.

- In a single summer afternoon in 1935, Jesse Owens broke four world records. He set or tied marks in the 100-yard dash, the 220-yard hurdles, the 220-yard dash, and the broad jump. Since then all of Jesse Owens' records have been bettered, but never has another athlete broken four records in a single day.
- A huge diamond of tremendous carat weight was taken to the finest cutter in Amsterdam. The entire value of the stone depended almost completely on the first cut. Needless to say, the diamond cutter felt the tremendous pressure of his task and spent a full month examining the stone to determine its natural cleavage. Finally the moment of truth arrived, and the diamond cutter raised his mallet to crack the massive diamond. But, when his cleaver hit the stone, the cleaver itself broke into two pieces. After collecting his wits again, the master cutter struck the stone again and was rewarded when

the stone split perfectly. He was so relieved he fainted on the floor.

- The story is told of an 81 year old man in Pontiac, Michigan, who keeps himself fit by climbing trees! One of his favorite show stoppers is to stand on his head in the crotch of a tree.

## More Facts

- Bulldogging is a popular rodeo event. In it, a cowboy on horseback chases after a steer. He then jumps from his horse, grabs the steer by the horns, then tries to wrestle the steer to the ground. But where did bulldogging get its name? One story claims that a famous cowboy, Bill Pickett, invented bulldogging. History says that Pickett used to grab his steer by the horns, but then he would bite the upper lip of the animal, letting go with his hands – just like a bulldog.

- Most people know that a dog pants to cool himself because he is incapable of sweating. However, dogs do sweat through the pads of their feet.

- If you were asked where the tallest pyramid on earth is located, would you answer San Francisco? The huge pyramid-shaped skyscraper that dominates the Bay area skyline exceeds even the massive height of the pyramids of Egypt.

- The workers at a bakery in Connecticut used to play a game at lunch time. They would play catch with a tin pie plate from the local bakery. The game became so popular that the idea was picked up commercially. Soon the disks were copied in plastic and embossed with the name of the pie company, "Frisbee."

- In ancient times, queens wore beards as a sign of royalty.

- The kangaroo got its name from Captain James Cook. When the English explorer was in Australia, he asked a native what the name of the strange, jumping animal was. The native replied, "Kangaroo." In his language it meant, "I don't know."

- India ink originally came from China.

- Most baseball players don't like being booed by people watching them play. But John "Boog" Powell of the Baltimore

Orioles said he didn't mind being booed. "After all," said Powell, "a boo is just three quarters of a Boog."

- You probably know that a group of bees is called a swarm and a group of cattle is called a herd. But did you know that a group of elk is called a gang? And did you know that several leopards are known as a leap? Other animal group names include a band of gorillas, a clowder (or a clutter) of cats, a knot of toad, a gaggle of geese, and a pride of lions.

- Poodle dogs originally came from Germany. The name "poodle" comes from the German word <u>pudel</u>, which means "to splash in water." The fancy breed that we now associate with pampered house pets was once a proud retriever and hunting dog.

- There is a six-foot-long dragon-like reptile in Australia called the goanna. In remote places where goannas and human rarely meet, the lizards have been known to mistake men for trees and attempt to climb them.

- In 1875 a horse race named the Kentucky Derby was run for the first time. A horse named Aristides won that race and earned a prize of $2,850. In 1974, the Kentucky Derby was run for the 100th time. A horse named Cannonade won and earned a prize of $274,000. So, in 100 years the winning prize has multiplied over 96 times.

- The cornerstone for the Washington Monument was laid in 1848. Over 20,000 people saw the beautiful 24,500-pound marble block put in place. However, it took 36 years to finish building the monument. And by that time the cornerstone had been covered up. Today no one knows exactly where the cornerstone is.

## The Final Fact

- During the Civil War, the town of Winchester, Virginia, belonged to both the North and the South. It changed hands a total of 68 times.

# Index

## N

## The Tidbits® Paper:

The Tidbits® paper was first published by Steele Media, Inc., in Billings, Montana in 1993. In 1994 it started its successful expansion across the country to what is now over one hundred forty areas. It is distributed not only to restaurants but also to grocery stores, doctors offices, convenience stores, oil change centers, anywhere people have time on their hands. Publishers of the Tidbits® paper earn income by sellling advertising that borders the text. For information on how you can become a publisher of the Tidbits® paper, call Steele Media, Inc. at 1-800-523-3096.

## Future Publications:

If you would like to be notified about future Tidbits® books and products contact Steele Media, Inc., P.O. Box 1255, Billings, MT 59103 (406) 248-9000 or 1-800-523-3096.